COUNT ON GOD

Discovery House
House
PUBLISHERS
BOX 3566 · GRAND RAPIDS, MI 49501

PUBLISHING BOOKS THAT FEED
THE SOUL WITH THE WORD OF GOD.

When your life doesn't add up . . .

COUNT
ON GOD

*Old Testament examples teach you to
depend on God's faithfulness*

James P. Keener

Count on God
Copyright © 1995 by James P. Keener

Discovery House Publishers is affiliated with
RBC Ministries, Grand Rapids, Michigan 49512

Discovery House books are distributed to the trade by
Thomas Nelson Publishers, Nashville, Tennessee 37214

All Scripture quotations are from the
New American Standard Bible.
Copyright © 1960, 1962, 1968, 1971, 1972
The Lockman Foundation. Used by permission.

Library of Congress Cataloging-in-Publication Data

Keener, James P.
      Count on God : Old Testament examples teach you to
   depend on God's faithfulness / James P. Keener.
         p.   cm.

   ISBN 0-929239-94-6

   1. Faith—Biblical teaching. 2. Christian life—Biblical
teaching. 3. Bible—Study and teaching. I. Title.
BS1199.F3K44   1995
234'.2—dc20   94-43714
                                                        CIP

Printed in the United States of America

95 96 97 98 99 / CHG / 10 9 8 7 6 5 4 3 2 1

Contents

Part III—*Living a Life That Counts*

Introduction

For a number of years I have wanted to write a book with a dedication that reads:

To my mother, who said, "When are you going to get a real job, Son?"
To my father, who said, "Don't you have to go to work soon?"
To my wife, who said, "Could we take a real vacation this year?"

I do not know that my mother, father, or wife actually said those things, but they probably thought them. You see, I am by profession a professor of mathematics, and as I suppose you know, mathematicians are an idiosyncratic bunch. In addition to wearing plastic pocket protectors, we tend to work unusual hours, have marginal social skills, and think that a mathematics conference in Detroit serves as an adequate site for a family vacation.

To make matters worse, at least in the eyes of my colleagues, I am a Christian. In addition to enjoying my profession, over the years I have developed a love for, and dedication to, understanding the Bible. As I have studied and learned more, I have led Bible studies and discussions, as well as adult Sunday school classes. But don't worry, there is no pressure on me to leave mathematics to become a television evangelist, because, to paraphrase Mark Twain, "He does not charge for his preaching, and he is worth every penny."

As I have learned more about the Bible and people, I have come to believe that many people do not know how to count. I am not referring here to a lack of mathematical ability, but rather to the fact that many people do not know what really matters in life. People do not know what to depend on to give meaning and purpose to life. They try all sorts of things, like multiple marriages, high-powered careers, luxury cars, sex, professional sports; yet they end up feeling empty. Surely, they hope, there is more to life than this.

Because we live in the same world, Christians are faced with the same choices as everyone else. The message of society is so loud that we often miss or are confused about the message of the Bible on what really matters in life. The prophet Elijah had to use drastic measures, such as a three-year drought and a dramatic demonstration of God's power over fire, to get the attention of the people, and to demonstrate conclusively that the gods they were worshiping were hopelessly incapable of fulfilling their promises. His challenge, "If the LORD is God, follow Him; but if Baal, follow him," is equally relevant today.

What follows is a collection of studies on what really counts in life. But rather than simply give you my opinion of the matter, I have drawn these studies from the biblical description of Old Testament characters, such as Abraham, Moses, Saul, David, and Jehoshaphat. It is my view that the Old Testament is a treasure trove of undiscovered wealth with great relevance for today. To be sure, some people have discovered this wealth, but to the vast majority of Christians, the Old Testament is either unknown or difficult to understand, and it is often viewed as nothing but long lists of hard-to-pronounce names. That was not the view of the apostle Paul. In his view,

Whatever was written in earlier times was written for our instruction, that through perseverance and the encouragement of the Scriptures we might have hope. (Romans 15:4)

These things [the events of the Old Testament] *happened to them as an example, and they were written for our instruction.* (1 Corinthians 10:11)

In the verses preceding this one, Paul makes it clear that the lessons we are to learn from the Israelites' experiences are spiritual in nature.

All ate the same spiritual food; and all drank the same spiritual drink, for they were drinking from a spiritual rock which followed them; and the rock was Christ. (1 Corinthians 10:3–4)

The real subject matter of the Old Testament is food for the spirit and the most important battles that were fought were those of spiritual significance. To understand the Old Testament solely on a historical, physical level is to miss its most important message. So the thrust of these studies is to see how the experiences of people of the Old Testament help us to live lives that count for something today.

"Creativity is undiscovered plagiarism" (William Inge, 1860–1954), or according to Solomon,

There is nothing new under the sun. Is there anything of which one might say, "See this, it is new"? Already it has existed for ages which were before us. (Ecclesiastes 1:9–11)

I do not believe that I have plagiarized anyone, but to deny that I have been influenced by other people would be a serious error. I have been greatly influenced in my thinking by the writings and sermons of Dr. Ray Stedman (Peninsula Bible Church, Palo Alto, California) and Dr. David Roper (Cole Community Church, Boise, Idaho). The teaching of these two men epitomizes to me the view that the Old Testament is of great relevance for today. Dr. Stedman's recent death ended an era of impact on many lives throughout the world. Perhaps, if you know these men's preaching and writing, you will see a similar conviction in these studies.

I also owe a debt of gratitude to the many people who have struggled with me in this task. Those in my Sunday school class have heard this material as it was being developed, and have been faithful in their support and encouragement. Phil Fischer was the one who let me know, in no uncertain terms, that I should quit making excuses and get serious about this project. He has continued to encourage me by reading the manuscript, providing important feedback, and praying for God's leading. Julie Fischer and Patty Horton put in many hours helping me develop the study guide and made numerous helpful suggestions along the way. I have gratefully accepted many ideas and suggestions from faithful friends, including John and Linda Tyson, Doug Lauffenberger, Fred Phelps, Cherry Wickel, and John Constance.

The contribution of my wife Kristine cannot be measured. It goes far beyond the cream cheese bagel and tea she often brings me when I am working in my study, or the luxury of free time that she provides me so that I may sit undisturbed at my cluttered desk, pace around the house with glassy eyes, or practice oral presentations while riding my bicycle, all under the designation of hard work. Maybe, now that this project is finished, we can take a real vacation.

Hints for Study Leaders

When I am in a bookstore looking at new books, whether or not a study guide is included at the end of each chapter is rarely a factor in determining if I should buy or read the book. There are plenty of good books that do not include study guides. Furthermore, I suspect that most people who read books do not take the time to work through their study guides.

On the other hand, if you are looking for a book to use for your Bible study group or for your Sunday school class, it may be that the first thing you look for is a book with a study guide. Leading a study or teaching a class is hard work, and anything you can find to help you is welcome.

As any student or teacher knows, reading for content is not the same as learning for life change. If there is anything I have learned in my years as a student and as a teacher, it is that I do not learn anything until I actively work through a topic on my own. I get only as much out of a study as I am willing to invest in hard work. Jesus expressed this principle when he said,

"Take care what you listen to. By your standard of measure it shall be measured to you; and more shall be given you besides. For whoever has, to him shall more be given; and whoever does not have, even what he has shall be taken away from him." (Mark 4:24–25)

Involving yourself in the learning process entails a number of things. For example, it includes reading with a pen or highlighter in hand, with notebook on your lap; Bible, concordance, and dictionary nearby. You may make notes in the margin, stop reading to find a related verse, or rewrite a key sentence in your own words. You may even get sidetracked onto a word study or character study that is only marginally mentioned in the text. You may find yourself asking your own questions and finding answers for them in your own words. You may even put down the book to call a friend or tell your spouse what you are learning. Learning is always enhanced when you are forced to express an idea clearly and concisely in your own words to someone else.

The study guide that follows each chapter was written to encourage this kind of participation, the kind that leads to genuine life change. There you will find questions about the content of the chapter, suggestions for additional study, questions of application, some specific action to take, and opportunities for personal commitment and response.

(Here is a project for you to do right now: Look up 2 Timothy 3:16 and list the four methods that Scripture uses to help us learn. How are these four different from each other?)

To take full advantage of this book and the study guide, I suggest that you incorporate the following:

• Encourage everyone in your class or study group to start a journal and to have a study partner to whom they will be accountable for their areas of personal commitment.

• Suggest that the participants read the passage of Scripture before they read the text. Encourage them to read with a pencil or highlighter in hand, taking notes as they go, with their Bible nearby.

• Get into the habit of personalizing the principles. In each chapter find specific ways in which you have experienced the truth of one of the principles, and encourage those in your study group to do the same. Do not rely solely on my experiences to shape your beliefs.

• Most of the suggestions for personal commitment are of two types: those denoted as "10-for-10" and those called "3-by-5." A 10-for-10 challenge calls for a commitment to a specific activity lasting ten minutes for ten days. A 3-by-5 challenge is to memorize a verse of

Scripture, which is made easier if it is written out on a 3" x 5" card and kept nearby for easy reference. You can aid in this process if, every time you meet as a group, you provide each member with a 3" x 5" card on which to write their personal commitment for the chapter.

• Some of the questions or projects are marked with an asterisk (*) as optional. You may want to assign these projects to your associate leader or to a member of the group one or two weeks ahead of time so that one person can do the project and report to others in the group what was learned.

• Be aware of projects that could benefit from your assistance. For example, for chapter 4 you might hand out copies of the words to some choruses or hymns, and you could sing them together to get the songs settled into the minds of the people in your group. For chapter 11, you might make a list of suggested projects that are more specific to your particular community.

Most of all, do not view what I have suggested here as the final word on anything. It is only a springboard for what I hope will be an exciting adventure in learning to count on God.

PART I

Learning To Count on God

The LORD is the one who goes ahead of you; He will be with you. He will not fail you or forsake you. Do not fear, or be dismayed.—Deuteronomy 31:8

1.

David Learns To Count

2 Samuel 24

He who leaves God out of the equation, does not know how to count.

"What do you do for a living, Mr. Keener?" It is a question that I am asked on a regular basis at social gatherings, and one I dread, because no matter how I respond, people will not comprehend the truth. If I say that I am a teacher, perhaps I am lying. I can confidently say that I am a lecturer, but whether I am a teacher or not depends on how much, if anything, my students learn. I suppose I could explain that I get paid to talk in other people's sleep. In times past I have responded that I am a ward of the state, or that I am a migrant worker (true, because I moved from one state-supported university to another), or that I am an example of your tax dollars at work.

If I respond with the accurate statement that I am a mathematics professor, I am often met with an incredulous, "Oh, that must be an interesting line of work." Most people have no idea at all of what a mathematician is paid to do, other than to teach more people to do the same. Sometimes I am asked if I know how to work story problems, and when I respond in the affirmative, it is somehow reassuring that at least I can do something useful. But it is essentially hopeless to indicate that I spend much of my time doing research in mathematics. "What can one research in mathematics?" or, "Aren't all the numbers already known?" are typical queries.

Perhaps you too suffer from math anxiety and are not quite sure why you are reading a book written by a math professor. Rest assured, this book is not about mathematics. But, it is about counting. You see, counting is more than putting numbers in the right order or giving a cardinal ordering to a collection of objects. Deep within everyone is a need to know what can be counted on in this life, and a cry that their own life will count for something significant, and this is not something that is usually taught in a mathematics class.

Like all of us, King David had to learn to count. His most important lesson on how to count came late in life, and it is recorded in 2 Samuel 24. We read,

The king said to Joab the commander of the army who was with him, "Go about now through all the tribes of Israel, from Dan to Beersheba, and register the people, that I may know the number of the people." (2 Samuel 24:2)

David wanted to count his people, so he ordered his commanding officer, Joab, to take a census. Joab was one of David's best friends, and he knew his king quite well. This request gave him an uneasy feeling that something was wrong, that there was a hidden agenda. He warned David not to pursue this census.

Joab said to the king, "Now may the LORD your God add to the people a hundred times as many as they are, while the eyes of my lord the king still see; but why does my lord the king delight in this thing?" (2 Samuel 24:3–4)

What could possibly be wrong with taking a simple census? After all, the information gained from a census has many potential uses. It could be used by the king to assess the needs and resources of his people and to develop programs that meet those needs. When he established the law for Israel, Moses did not forbid taking a census, but rather he provided guidelines on how to conduct one. He wrote,

When you take a census of the sons of Israel to number them . . . ."
*(*Exodus 30:12)

Yet, as soon as the census was completed, David knew that he had done something seriously wrong.

David's heart troubled him after he had numbered the people. So David said to the LORD, "I have sinned greatly in what I have done."
(2 Samuel 24:10)

What had David done wrong? Where was the sin in what he had done? The clue to the problem with this census is found in the final report that Joab presented to David.

*Joab gave the number of the registration of the people to the king; and there were in Israel eight hundred thousand valiant men who drew the sword, and the men of Judah were five hundred thousand men. (2 Samuel 24:9)

The goal of David's census was to determine the size and strength of his army and his reserve fighting force. He had no interest at all in the size of the rest of the population. He was not concerned with the educational system, to know if there were adequate facilities and teachers for their young children, if the needs of senior citizens were being met, or if the poor were adequately housed and fed. David simply wanted to know how strong he was.

How often we do the same when we try to determine our areas of strength, in order to convince ourselves that we are better or stronger than someone else. This happens in the department where I work, because everyone in the department has his or her list of the top researchers or best lecturers in the department. We count journal publications, published books, citations by other workers, invitations to speak at other universities, and research funding, to assess a person's "strength" as a mathematician.

This kind of "census taking" occurs just about everywhere. In churches, we count the size of our congregations to determine who has the best church or most dynamic preacher. Retailers count to see which stores move the most goods. Bank officials count to see which bank has the largest assets. Salesmen count to see who receives the highest commissions. On a recent cross-country flight, I overheard a salesman complaining that because of the success of a younger colleague, he had slipped to number four in sales in his company. Everywhere we turn, someone is counting to see how strong or important they are.

The apostle Paul was quite explicit in denouncing "census taking" for the purpose of comparing strength.

We are not bold to class or compare ourselves with some of those who commend themselves; but when they measure themselves by themselves, and compare themselves with themselves, they are without understanding. (2 Corinthians 10:12)

According to Paul, people who base their opinion of themselves on how they compare with other people are clueless about what really matters—they do not know how to count.

I recently bought a computer program that keeps track of my financial records and writes checks to pay my bills at home. The program has a number of helpful features, including the ability to prepare reports about cash flow, outstanding bills, and the like. One report I have come to dislike, however, is the "net worth" report. There on one page I can see all of my financial assets and liabilities. In my case, there is not much worth in my net; but other more financially successful people may feel rather smug about their worth. Therein lies the problem.

Too often in our society we summarize our strengths or weaknesses in terms of our net worth, whether it be monetary resources, intellectual ability, communication skills, quick-wittedness, or athletic ability. By determining my worth in these terms, I am making the same mistake made by David when he acted as if his strength depended on the size of his army.

David knew, or was supposed to know, that his true strength was not based on the size of his army, but on the size of his God. This is a clear message of the Old Testament: that it is God who would fight Israel's battles, and no army of any size could stand against the force of their awesome God. The king of Israel was supposed to know this. The Israelites were told that when they selected a king,

"You shall surely set a king over you whom the LORD *your God chooses, one from among your countrymen . . . . Moreover, he shall not multiply horses for himself, nor shall he cause the people to return to Egypt to multiply horses, since the* LORD *has said to you, 'You shall never again return that way.' "* (Deuteronomy 17:15–16)

For the Egyptians and the Assyrians, horses were prized possessions and were important in warfare, but it was supposed to be different for Israel. The prophet Isaiah stated succinctly what was wrong with multiplying horses or going back to Egypt.

Woe to those who go down to Egypt for help, and rely on horses, and trust in chariots because they are many, and in horsemen because they are very strong, but they do not look to the Holy One of Israel, nor seek the LORD*! . . . The Egyptians are men, and not God, and their horses are flesh and not spirit.* (Isaiah 31:1, 3)

At a different time, David wrote the following lines,

Some boast in chariots, and some in horses; but we will boast in the name of the LORD*, our God.* (Psalm 20:7)

In other words, it is both wrong and foolish to place our reliance on physical might, such as large armies or horses and chariots, or other aspects of our "flesh" like intellect, financial acumen, or athletic ability. David needed to *learn to count on God's resources to fight his battles.*

David was not alone in this need. Gideon (in Judges 6–7) had to learn this lesson in dramatic fashion. Gideon began his encounter with the Midianites with a recruited army of 32,000 men. Frankly, if the battle were to be fought by traditional methods without God's intervention, this would not have been enough men anyway. The forces of the Midianites numbered 120,000, and they were very effective fighters, having discovered the military superiority of camels in the desert for marauding warfare. But God instructed Gideon to pare his army down to a paltry three hundred men.

The LORD said to Gideon, "The people who are with you are too many for Me to give Midian into their hands, lest Israel become boastful, saying, 'My own power has delivered me.' " (Judges 7:2)

When we experience success, we often think it is because we are clever, strong, or persuasive. If I win an argument, or if a class I lead is well received by students, how easy it is for me to conclude that it was because I am such a great orator or teacher, and that my abilities have earned for me my success. Gideon had to be taught that such an explanation was totally without foundation. It is not my power or ability that gives victory, it is God's.

By ordering the census, David had made a serious mistake, and he admitted that he had "acted very foolishly." His admission was accurate, but it did not prevent the need for discipline, and seventy thousand people died from a pestilence sent by God. The text (2 Samuel 24:1) tells us that the people were not totally innocent, but nonetheless, this was a terrible thing to happen, and to our way of thinking, it seems unrelated and out of proportion to David's sin. But David had to learn the second important lesson: that you can *always count on the consequences of sin.*

Many of the terrible things that happen in our society are the consequences of the fact that we live in a fallen world. Many people act as if their personal decisions have no future consequences and will not affect other people. Popular phrases like "Just do it!" and "Go for it!" promote the lie that we can live as we please. How many fathers or mothers fail to realize the terrible effects on the lives of their children when they move every three years just to keep advancing on the career ladder, or when they seek a new spouse because "I've gotta be me." Children are affected by the consequences of their parents' acts just as nations are affected by the mistakes of their leaders. Some sins that seem insignificant at the time can have disastrous long-term implications, and rarely, if ever, are we able to comprehend the complicated cause-and-effect relationships between sin and its consequences. But the fact remains that sin always has consequences, both for the individual sinner and for many uninvolved bystanders, both now and for the future.

In the process of sorting through his sin, David made an amazing statement.

David said to Gad, "I am in great distress. Let us now fall into the hand of the LORD for His mercies are great, but do not let me fall into the hand of man." (2 Samuel 24:14)

David recognized that a sinner in the hands of an angry God has more reason for hope than does offending man in the clutches of an offended society. Society's laws are nebulous and the meting of justice is capricious. Consider, for example, the Rodney King trials in Los Angeles. In the first trial all police officers were acquitted; in the second, two were found guilty. The facts in the case had not changed, but the verdict changed. At times in the past, people in Western cultures have been beheaded for crimes that today are completely ignored, and there are no guarantees that society will not swing back to its earlier ways at some time in the future.

The fundamental difficulty with our society's legal system is that we have appointed men to be judges. There are four qualifications that a judge should have. He should be appointed to the position, he should have full knowledge of the law, he should have full access to the facts, and he should be completely unbiased in his decisions. There is not a single human being who qualifies on all four counts. In contrast, God is the righteous Judge, and we can trust His judgments to be correct. Yet, if we have any sense at all, that is not what we want, because we know that if we received exactly what we deserved, we would be in serious trouble. Every person alive has a moral code and lives in constant violation of it, thereby admitting that they are deserving of judgment. Tolstoy wrote that "man's whole life is a continual contradiction of what he knows to be his duty. In every department of life he acts in defiant opposition to the dictates of his conscience and common sense."

Most people hope to avoid getting what they know they deserve by maneuvering for a lenient judge, trying to confuse or justify the evidence, or hoping for a hung jury or mistrial on a technicality. These tactics do not work with God. The only reasonable approach is to throw ourselves at the mercy of God and, in open admission of our guilt, ask for His forgiveness. At the same time that He is the righteous Judge, God is the loving and merciful Father, and we need to learn to *count on the love and mercy of God.*

This attitude is in stark contrast to the common attitude toward pagan gods. The pagan gods, the gods of man's imagination, are vengeful and capricious, not loving and gracious. They are distant and impersonal, easily angered, and not readily appeased.

But because David knew his God, he understood the process of restoration, of coming back into a close relationship with God that had been broken when he had sinned. David was told to erect an altar on the threshing floor of a Jebusite named Araunah. Because David was the king, he could have taken the property from Araunah by force, or he could have accepted it as a gift, since the property, as well as the oxen, their threshing sledges, and their yokes were offered to him by Araunah as a gift for a burnt offering.

David's response is noteworthy:

> *The king said to Araunah, "No, but I will surely buy it from you for a price, for I will not offer burnt offerings to the LORD my God which cost me nothing." (2 Samuel 24:24)*

From 1 Chronicles 21:25 and 2 Samuel 24:24 we know that David paid the fair market value of six hundred shekels of gold for the land and fifty shekels of silver for the threshing floor and the oxen. To David, the actual amount of money was inconsequential, and it certainly did not create a hardship. Yet, by paying for the property, David demonstrated that he understood that his relationship with God had true worth.

It was not possible for David to bribe God or to buy His forgiveness, and neither is it possible for us. No amount of good deeds can make us worthy of God's mercy. No amount of money can compare to the infinite worth of knowing Christ. Yet, for the follower of God, a disciple of Jesus Christ, there is a cost. If we want to experience the value of a genuine, vibrant relationship with an awesome God, there is a price to pay, with our time, our talents, and our treasure.

This cost is easy to understand in terms of family relationships. No matter how appropriate the words or picture, I would never give my wife a birthday or anniversary card that someone else previously gave to me, with the original signature erased or scratched out and replaced with my own. And neither would you. Somehow, your claims of love do not ring true if you never give something to your spouse that is of value to you, or if the two of you never carve time out of your busy schedules to be alone together. However, if you are truly in love, self-sacrifice is spontaneous and barely noticed because of the satisfaction you receive from bringing joy to the one you love. This cost does not create a hardship, but comes simply as an expression of a heart that understands the "fair market value" of a loving relationship. As Christ himself made it clear, His followers must learn to *count the cost of relationship.*

So this is the program for learning how to count. If you want your life to count for something, you must learn, as did David,

1) to count on God's resources,
2) to count on the consequences of sin,
3) to count on God's love and mercy,
4) to count the cost of relationship.

There is not much prestige for a university professor who must teach remedial algebra. We professors take pride in the marvelous advanced topics that we have mastered, and the knowledge with which we can dazzle our students. Certainly, we would scoff at someone who asks, "But, do you know how to count?" Yet, for many highly educated people, if the question is, "Do you know what can be truly counted on in life?" the honest answer is, "No."

For the Christian, learning to count means knowing how to answer these three questions:

• Have you come to realize that God is bigger than any of the difficulties you face, and do you count on Him to lead you and to fight your battles for you?

• Do you understand that God is both just and merciful, and do these dual characteristics of God guide and constrain your daily decisions?

• Do you know how to maintain a personal relationship with God, and does that relationship give meaning and purpose to your life?

Study Guide for Chapter 1

1. For content:
• Read 2 Samuel 24.

• Write in your own words a summary of the four main points of chapter 1 of this book.

• It is popular today to proclaim that people need more self-confidence. Is this consistent with the ideas expressed in this chapter? Why or why not?

* Read Judges 6–7. Was Gideon a self-confident man? What was his source of strength?

2. For further study:
• Find five different verses in the Psalms that use the word *strength*. (There are well over fifty such verses. For example, read Psalm 18, Psalm 28, Psalm 31, or Psalm 84.) What is the theme that summarizes the main idea of these verses?

• What was the apostle Paul's attitude toward his weaknesses, as expressed in 2 Corinthians 12:9–10?

* How is the strength of God depicted in Job 38 and 39?

3. For application:
• Make an honest assessment of where you are in relationship to the four main points of this chapter.

• What are some of your strengths, and what are some of your liabilities?

• What are some of your weaknesses, and how can God use them?

4. For action:
To help remind you that there is a cost to maintaining a relationship, do something kind, totally unexpected, and totally without the possibility of payback, for some friends (for example, mow their lawn when they are away from home, or give an anonymous gift certificate for books from your local Christian book store).

5. For personal commitment:
10-for-10: Commit yourself to reading the Bible for ten minutes every day for the next ten days. If you are not sure where to begin, read a few chapters from the book of Psalms or Proverbs. This will not necessarily be convenient or fit nicely into your schedule, but spending time reading God's Word is crucial to building a relationship with God that adds up.

2.

Fighting a Holy War

Deuteronomy 7

Most of the people that I know are "normal" people with "normal" problems. Students want to know what course to take next year, what they must learn in order to get a "C," what to do about Professor X who is a rotten lecturer, what to do with a background in art appreciation, how to find a spouse, or how to assure a successful career.

My friends at church want to know how to work for a demanding boss, how to live with a non-Christian spouse, how to adjust to being a single parent, how to teach teenagers to avoid drugs or premarital sex, what to do if the lump is malignant, or how to supplement Social Security income for a comfortable retirement. Do the promises of God have any relevance for ordinary people like us?

By comparison, the uncertainties facing Moses and the nation of Israel seemed overwhelming. They were a ragtag bunch of runaway slaves, refugees living in a barren wilderness, with no military training or equipment, and no natural resources on which to draw. Canaan, the land to which they were headed, was inhabited by strong and ruthless people, some of whom were giants. They appeared to be marching toward certain annihilation. Yet the promise of God was that they were going to overthrow the inhabitants and possess the land.

*"When the LORD your God shall bring you into the land where
you are entering to possess it, and shall clear away many nations before you, the Hittites and the Girgashites and the Amorites and the
Canaanites and the Perizzites and the Hivites and the Jebusites, seven
nations greater and stronger than you . . . ."* (Deuteronomy 7:1)

People today do not concern themselves with how to fight Hittites,
Girgashites, Amorites, Canaanites, Perizzites, Hivites, and Jebusites.
The enemies we face are called by different names. We worry about
our own problems, like how to pay the bills, what to do about a broken
relationship or a rebellious child, or how to find a better job. The enemies we face are primarily spiritual rather than physical in nature, because they affect our spirits much more than our bodies. You may get
your children to eat their vegetables or do their homework, but the
struggle is for them to do these willingly. The real battle is a battle of
wills. Feelings of anger, anxiety, impatience, inconsistency, discouragement, depression, pride, greed, or lust are evidences of a spiritual
conflict. The apostle Paul expressed the fact that ours is a spiritual
conflict:

*Our struggle is not against flesh and blood, but against the rulers,
against the powers, against the world-forces of this darkness, against
the spiritual forces of wickedness in the heavenly places.* (Ephesians
6:12)

Physicists have identified the four fundamental forces of nature to
be the strong and weak nuclear forces, the electromagnetic force, and
the gravitational force. These forces are identified and recognized by
their actions and realms of influence. For example, no one has ever
seen gravity, rather we have seen the effect of gravity as it acts to pull
together two massive objects. The light from a light bulb is evidence
that the electromagnetic force is active, but you cannot see the force
that is moving electrons through the light bulb's filament. The effect
of a force or power is to move the objects under its influence.

Similarly a spiritual force or power can be recognized by its action and realm of influence. The action of spiritual forces of wickedness are observed as the influences or pressures that are applied to attempt to move our spirits away from a relationship of trust and dependence on God. The battle with spiritual forces and powers is for movement of the mind, and it is fought in the realm of desires, ideas, attitudes, feelings, opinions, thoughts, and beliefs.

The evidences that there are spiritual forces at work, trying to influence or move us, are easy to spot. When you walk into a crowded arena before a sports event, you may sense a spirit or atmosphere of bitter competition; in a business board room there may be a spirit of fierce intensity; in the coffee room at work there may be a spirit of gloom, despondency, or jealousy; or in a crowd of picketers there may be an atmosphere of anger. At professional sporting events, there is a deliberate attempt to control the emotions of the fans, while advertisers use psychological tools to convince us to buy their products. In these settings people often take on a different spirit, a crowd mentality, a corporate personality, or a form of schizophrenia, as they behave in ways that they would not consider acceptable in a different setting. Grown men become angry or verbally abusive. We say things for which we are later ashamed (or should be) and we buy things for which we have no use. When we say that we just "got carried away," we are admitting that we were moved by the dominant influence of the place.

In these environments, there is spiritual pressure that is pushing us into a particular mode of thinking or reacting, attempting to discredit trust in God and His ability to provide for our every need. The aim of these influences is for you to believe that your sports team, your boss, your possessions, can provide an emotional high, some needed determination, or a feeling of acceptance and importance—something that, at the moment, you believe God cannot provide. Their goal is accomplished when you disrespect God by honoring and admiring these other things more than God.

The fundamental problem is not with your boss, your team, your possessions; the problem goes beyond these. This is what the apostle

Paul explained in 1 Corinthians 10:19–20 when he said,

"What do I mean then? That a thing sacrificed to idols is any-thing, or that an idol is anything? No, but I say that the things which the Gentiles sacrifice, they sacrifice to demons, and not to God."

In Paul's day there were temples filled with idols that were hon-ored in religious ritual. The idols and temples of worship of our mod-ern secular society are less obviously religious, largely because their pursuit does not include formalized rituals, and is not given tax-ex-empt status by the IRS. Worship is simply the act of ascribing value to something by giving it honor and recognition. Idolatry is the act of at-tributing to something a higher value than it deserves, at the expense of not attributing to God His true worth.

One might worship or idolize an expensive car, but according to Paul, the car and the monetary sacrifices made to own that car are insignificant. Instead, the real problem is that the sacrifices that one makes to own an expensive car are made because of the implicit be-lief that the car will give its owner importance, significance, or no-toriety.

One might be infatuated with literature, magazines, or videos having explicit sexual content. According to Paul, the monetary sacri-fices made to purchase or rent these objects are actually sacrifices to the spirit or fantasy portrayed by the magazine or movie suggesting that true satisfaction comes by seeking an extramarital affair or sex as recreation.

The object of worship itself is insignificant. Paul called the ideas behind these objects "demons," and it is they who can possess and dominate your life. It is against these influences and forces that the real battle is fought.

If the battle were of a physical nature, we would understand how to fight it. Our government and our entertainment industry have taught us quite well how to use physical power to overcome an enemy. Ac-cording to their example, we should buy the appropriate weapon and blast the enemy into oblivion. But the Christian is told that his battles, which are mostly spiritual, are not to be fought using physical methods.

> *Though we walk in the flesh, we do not war according to the flesh, for the weapons of our warfare are not of the flesh, but divinely powerful for the destruction of fortresses.* (2 Corinthians 10:3–4)

Even though Moses knew that the Israelites had to face specific physical enemies, their battles had a substantial spiritual component, and in Deuteronomy 7, Moses left instructions for how to wage Holy War. His instructions are equally relevant for us today.

The first part of the instruction related to attitudes toward the enemy:

> *"When the LORD your God shall deliver them before you, and you shall defeat them, then you shall utterly destroy them. You shall make no covenant with them and show no favor to them. Furthermore, you shall not intermarry with them; you shall not give your daughters to their sons, nor shall you take their daughters for your sons. For they will turn your sons away from following Me to serve other gods; then the anger of the LORD will be kindled against you, and He will quickly destroy you. But thus you shall do to them: you shall tear down their altars, and smash their sacred pillars, and hew down their Asherim, and burn their graven images with fire."* (Deuteronomy 7:2–5)

Moses' instruction is summarized well by the phrase *"be utterly ruthless against the enemy's influence."* If we wish to have victory over our spiritual enemies, we must be absolutely ruthless, not allowing compromise to weaken our position in any way. The purpose of a covenant or intermarriage is to gain political or economic advantage without a struggle. As we will see in chapter 7 from the example of Joshua with the people of Gibeon (Joshua 9), we lose much more than we gain when we make compromises. You see, compromise gives recognition to other gods, be they gods of beauty, wealth, or popularity. When we make covenants we buy into the system of the enemy, and we give it a credence that it does not deserve. It does not take long before our servitude is to the gods of this world. This is what happened to Solomon when he failed to heed the command not to intermarry.

It came about when Solomon was old, his wives turned his heart away after other gods; and his heart was not wholly devoted to the LORD his God, as the heart of David his father had been. (1 Kings 11:4)

Just as the gods in Moses' day, the gods of today's world have reminders of worship strategically placed throughout our society. They too have altars, pillars, Asherim, and graven images. Altars are places where we make sacrifices in order to keep peace with our god (shopping malls and credit card companies?). Pillars were symbols of power and strength and were sometimes named. For example, the two main pillars of Solomon's temple were named Jachin, meaning "he shall establish," and Boaz, meaning "in it is strength." Today our symbols of power and strength are called by foreign names such as Mercedes and Porsche. In Moses' day, Asherim were symbols of female deities, intended to arouse lust. Today, Asherim are the constant reminders of our desires that appear on billboards, in magazines, and on TV advertisements. Graven images are objects to which we look for inspiration (motivational seminars?). The magazines we read, the music we listen to, the TV programs and movies we watch, and perhaps some of the friends we hang out with, promote the belief that there is something we need and can have that our loving Father, Almighty God, cannot or will not provide. We cannot eliminate these things from our society, but the command of Moses is clear: Be utterly ruthless in ridding your life of evil influences.

So the first instruction from Moses on fighting a holy war is to *maintain a lifestyle that prevents infiltration by the enemy.*

If you think practically about this for a minute, you may have a few reactions, like, "Does this mean I can't use credit cards?" or,

"Must I get rid of the television? Surely you don't want me to give up Monday Night Football!"

When faced with the prospect of radical lifestyle changes that diminish the world's influence on us, such as living without debt, or taking a lower paying job that allows more time at home, most people I know are flooded with questions that begin with, "But what if . . . ?" or, "But how will I . . . ?" indicating fear of leaving behind their source of security, or a fear of the unknown. Because I have chosen to send my children to a Christian school, I must depend for yet another year on my noisy, worn-out excuse for a car. I live with the uncertainty of not knowing where it will breakdown, and of having no contingency plans for when it does.

Moses knew that the Israelites would have similar fears.

"If you should say in your heart, 'These nations are greater than I; how can I dispossess them?' you shall not be afraid of them." (Deuteronomy 7:17–18)

The biggest obstacle we face in our spiritual battle is fear, and we must *learn how to overcome fear.* Fear was certainly the most difficult thing for Gideon to overcome in his confrontation of the Midianites, and fear was the weapon that God used to destroy the Midianites. As we saw in Desert Storm, when an army becomes afraid, it loses its will and ability to fight, and the battle is over.

Fear keeps many people from doing what they know they should do as they are faced with threatening questions or situations. "What if I lose the argument? What if I am wrong? What if this does not work? What if I lose my job? What if people laugh at me or ridicule me?"

The key to getting rid of our fear is to *build our confidence in God.* Moses identifies three ways that our confidence in God is established.

"You shall not be afraid of them; you shall well remember what the LORD your God did to Pharaoh and to all Egypt: the great trials which your eyes saw and the signs and the wonders and the mighty

hand and the outstretched arm by which the LORD your God brought you out. So shall the LORD your God do to all the peoples of whom you are afraid." (Deuteronomy 7:18–19)

We overcome our fear by *reminding ourselves of what God has done in the past*, and using this as a reminder that God is in control of the events of human history, including those that affect us personally. This is why the nation of Israel was encouraged to build memorials.

"Let this be a sign among you, so that when your children ask you later, saying, 'What do these stones mean to you?' then you shall say to them, 'Because the waters of the Jordan were cut off before the ark of the covenant of the LORD; when it crossed the Jordan, the waters of the Jordan were cut off.' So these stones shall become a memorial to the sons of Israel forever." (Joshua 4:6–7)

We need to be creating and keeping godly memories for ourselves, our children, and grandchildren. Christians may write in journals or scrapbooks, or make notes in their Bibles, but we all need reminders of how God has worked in the world and in our lives. My notes contain numerous reminders of God's leading in my life. I can point to His specific leading regarding my university training and my first "real" job search. When my children ask, "Dad, how did you know that Mom was the right person for you to marry?" I have a ready answer of how God led me.

We also overcome fear when we *avoid comparing our own strength with the strength of the enemy*. When our focus is on comparison with the enemy, the problems always seem so large, and we feel outnumbered, facing an impossible task. Instead, we should learn to compare the enemy to our awesome God, and having done so, realize that the enemy is in serious trouble, not we.

"You shall not dread them, for the LORD your God is in your midst, a great and awesome God." (Deuteronomy 7:21)

Finally, we overcome fear when we learn to *recognize how God works*. Since God does not fight the same way we would fight, it is often difficult to recognize when and how God is at work. Moses lists two weapons that God uses to fight a battle. First, Moses said that when the Israelites were in battle,

" . . . the LORD your God will send the hornet against them." (Deuteronomy 7:20)

One way God puts the enemy into disarray is through "acts of God," that is, "natural" occurrences over which people have absolutely no control. "Sending the hornet" is one example of the kinds of things that God can use to demonstrate our impotence. In addition to swarming insects and pestilence, God can use drought, famine, plague, sickness, earthquakes, flash floods, and windstorms. Against Jericho (according to archaeological data), God used a series of earthquakes, one of which initiated a landslide that blocked the Jordan upstream at Adam, so that the Israelites could cross the Jordan at Gilgal. Against Sisera God used a flash flood (Judges 4–5). Against the Philistines He used a swarm of insects in the bushes that sounded from a distance like an approaching army (2 Samuel 5). Against Ahab He used a drought (1 Kings 18). For the Moabites the morning sun reflecting off of muddy water looked like blood and gave them the false impression that the Israelites had self-destructed (2 Kings 3). Even today, God can use devastating hurricanes, earthquakes, floods, and rampaging fires to get people's attention.

At other times God has used spiritual weapons against our enemies.

The LORD your God shall deliver them before you, and will throw them into great confusion until they are destroyed. (Deuteronomy 7:23)

In times past, God has used confusing rumors, economic depression, and political upheaval. Against 120,000 Midianites (Judges 6–7), and against a million Ethiopians (2 Chronicles 14), God used fear. Against Rabshakeh (2 Kings 19), He used a rumor that a foreign army would attack. In his description of how God was going to use Cyrus, king of Persia, to accomplish His purposes for Judah, Isaiah described how God works.

"For the sake of Jacob My servant, and Israel My chosen one, I have also called you by your name; I have given you a title of honor though you have not known Me. I am the LORD, and there is no other; the One forming light and creating darkness, causing well-being and creating calamity; I am the LORD who does all these." (Isaiah 45:4–5a, 7)

In other words, even though Cyrus did not recognize God's hand in the matter, He was determining the conditions, be they peaceful or calamitous, that led to the rise and fall of leaders, regimes, and governments. Today as well, God is able to bring about the collapse of regimes where billions of dollars of U.S. defense expenditures are ineffective, even counterproductive. He is able to frustrate the best-laid plans of the most qualified and organized people.

"I will also break down your pride of power; I will also make your sky like iron and your earth like bronze. And your strength shall be spent uselessly, for your land shall not yield its produce and the trees of the land shall not yield their fruit." (Leviticus 26:19–20)

During difficult times, such as after a devastating accident, the loss of a loved one, or an injury or extended illness, people are forced to question the basis of their hope for a secure future. It is during these times of questioning and searching that they realize the inadequacy of their reliance. God fights His battles by directly attacking those "sure" things upon which we have come to rely.

By remembering God's victories in the past, by seeing His superiority to the enemy, and by recognizing the techniques He uses, we come to have confidence that victory is assured and our fear is overcome.

I still remember driving into Pasadena, California, approaching the campus where I was to begin graduate study. Moving slowly past buildings where scientific giants like Millikan, Einstein, and Feynman had worked struck terror in my heart. I knew that only the very best students went to Caltech, and all I could ask myself was, "What in the world am I doing here?"

I had much more modest plans for myself. My undergraduate grades were good but not great, so I applied only to those graduate schools where I believed I had a realistic chance of being accepted. A few faculty members suggested that the best place for someone with my interests to study was Caltech, but the chances of my being able to attend there were slim to none. One instructor bluntly told me that to apply there would be a total waste of my time. I applied to Caltech for only one reason: There was no application fee, so what could I lose?

I had already decided that I wanted to study at another university. It was a fine university and study there was by no means a trivial goal, yet I was (self) confident that this was achievable. I did not realize that God had arranged otherwise.

A number of graduate schools had an agreement to make offers of financial aid on the same week in March so that all acceptance decisions could be made within a two-week span. On the fateful day when first-offer letters arrived, I received two offers, a full fellowship to Caltech, and an offer of partial aid requiring substantial teaching hours from the school of my dreams.

I was an emotional mess. The offer from Caltech was totally unexpected and I had no confidence that I could succeed there. The second offer, where I was certain I would be accepted and where I wanted to go, was inadequate to meet my barest financial necessities.

In conversation with faculty advisors over the next few days, I decided to give Caltech a try. After all, I did not have any other realistic offers. During this time, however, another professor was trying desperately (I learned later) to contact me to encourage me to hold off on

my decision. The modesty of their offer was the result of an adminis-
trative foul-up, and he was confident that money from other sources
was forthcoming to upgrade my offer to a full three-year fellowship.
But for some Unknown Reason, as hard as he tried, he could not get
through to me.

Only a few hours after I dropped my letter of acceptance to
Caltech into the mailbox, I received his telegram pleading with me to
wait—but it was too late. A week later I had in hand the offer that I
had originally wanted, but God had decided to send me to Caltech.

Six months later as I was driving in trepidation along California
Boulevard, I needed to recall that pivotal week in March, when God
taught me that He is in control of all of the uncontrollable events in
my life.

The second obstacle we face in the battle against spiritual enemies
is dealing with *unrealistic expectations.* It is natural to think that since
God is all-powerful, He should solve our problems for us right away.
But that is not His method, and that is not what we should expect.

*"The LORD your God will clear away these nations before you lit-
tle by little; you will not be able to put an end to them quickly, lest the
wild beasts grow too numerous for you."* (Deuteronomy 7:22)

*"I will not drive them out before you in a single year, that the land
may not become desolate, and the beasts of the field become too numerous for you. I will drive them out before you little by little, until you
become fruitful and take possession of the land."* (Exodus 23:29–30)

Wouldn't it be nice if we could be zapped and our anger, pride, anxiety, discouragement, and lust were taken away all at once? With one
touch, my colleagues would all become tolerable, my children would
become responsible, and my students would become serious about
their studies. Moses said that no, this is not the desirable method, but
that victory comes little by little, one skirmish at a time. The danger,
according to Moses, is that if every problem were taken out of our lives

at once, there would not be enough good disciplines to fill the voids, so that other, more difficult problems would creep in to replace the old ones and we would be worse off than before. Instead, as we gradually become fruitful in different areas of our lives, as we develop godly disciplines and as God's Spirit gains control of our nature, our fruitfulness drives out problem areas for which there is no longer any room.

This is how farmers in the American West make the wilderness bloom. They clear sagebrush, install irrigation equipment and fencing, and begin cultivating a modest patch of land. As one piece of land becomes productive, they increase the size of their operation by clearing an adjacent piece of land, and so on. If they bite off too big a chunk at one time, they lose control of the land they have, and soon coyotes are killing their lambs, deer and elk are wintering on their newly sown fields, and sagebrush is reappearing on their pasture.

I find it reassuring to learn that, according to Acts 13:19, it took four hundred fifty years for God's promise to Moses to be fulfilled with the establishment of David's kingdom. This gives me a better framework in which to understand that God is dealing with me gradually, yet thoroughly.

I am confident of this very thing, that He who began a good work in you will perfect it until the day of Christ Jesus. (Philippians 1:6)

The third obstacle we face in dealing with our spiritual enemies is *regression,* that is, allowing old habits or memories to be reawakened and falling back into old patterns after a victory has been won.

"The graven images of their gods you are to burn with fire; you shall not covet the silver or the gold that is on them, nor take it for yourselves, lest you be snared by it, for it is an abomination to the LORD your God." (Deuteronomy 7:25)

After victory is secured, it is easy to let little things that remind us of the world's gods creep back into our lives. Moses mentions graven images, but for us it might be magazines, TV programs, or rented videos that we allow back into our homes, that reawaken old desires or old habits, or former friends whose influence on us is not positive. The command of Moses is clear. Just as we must be ruthless against these influences before the battle, so too we must remain ruthlessly opposed to these influences after the victory is apparently won. It is too easy to regress, and lose the ground that was so difficult to win.

So these are Moses' instructions on how to fight a holy war. His advice is:

1) to be ruthlessly opposed to enemy infiltration and influence,
2) to overcome fear,
3) to avoid unrealistic expectations,
4) to avoid regression after victory is won.

We overcome our fear
    a) by reminding ourselves of God's faithfulness in the past,
    b) by comparing the enemy to God and not to ourselves,
    c) by observing how God is at work in the world.

Notice that there is one glaring omission in this list: Nowhere in these instructions does Moses describe detailed military tactics. Similarly, in Deuteronomy 20, another passage in which Moses describes how to prepare for a holy war, nowhere is there instruction on the tactics of war. The reason for this omission is apparent. The instruction is not intended to help us fight the battle by ourselves, but rather it is to teach us

5) to rely on God to fight the battle.

The primary problem we face is that of misplaced allegiance and dependence. The emphasis of Moses' teaching is to help us count on God's resources to fight our battles.

The lesson for us should be clear. God has offered to fight our spiritual battles for us. He does not want us to live lives that are defeated by spiritual enemies, producing in us anger, frustration, anxiety, discouragement, pride, laziness, rebellion, greed, or lust. He has shown us repeatedly that He is trustworthy and we have nothing to fear when we place our trust entirely in Him.

Study Guide for Chapter 2

1. For content:
• Read Deuteronomy 7.

• What are some of the instructions found in Deuteronomy 7, and what are some of the promises that result if these instructions are followed?

• What attitude of idolatry is being promoted by the "spirit" of the following?
    The fashion industry,
    The beverage industry,
    The entertainment industry,
    The life insurance industry,
    The sports industry.

• What was the secret weapon with which Gideon defeated the Midianites in Judges 7:19–22?

2. For further study:
• What one phrase is repeated in the following verses: Genesis 50:19–21; Deuteronomy 20:1, 3–4; Joshua 11:6; 1 Samuel 23:16–18; 2 Kings 1:15; Nehemiah 4:14? What is the common theme in these verses?

• What emotions do you imagine the young man in Mark 10:17–22 felt when Jesus told him that he had to sell everything that he had?

• According to Colossians 2:8, what can take us into captivity? How?

3. For application:
• Make a list of some of the spiritual struggles you face (like anger, boredom, frustration, jealousy, fear of disapproval). Can you identify the battleground for these struggles; that is, where, when, or in what

situations are these struggles most likely to take place for you? Are there specific changes you can make in your lifestyle to rid yourself of these influences?

• Why is fear such a powerful weapon? Are there areas of your life that are dominated by fear? What are its consequences?

• What "secret weapons" do you, as a Christian, have to combat the powerful influences of idolatry?

• What is the "secret of contentment" that the apostle Paul had (Philippians 4:11–13)?

4. For action:
• Start a notebook or scrapbook, keeping track of important events and experiences in your Christian life. Include pictures of your prayer partners, copies of verses or songs that are especially meaningful to you, notes of encouragement that you have received, or other reminders of the ways that God is working in your life.

* Go to a library and read the article by Amos Nur in *The New Scientist,* July 6, 1991, pp. 45–48, on earthquakes in the Holy Land.

5. For personal commitment:
3-by-5: Memorize Deuteronomy 7:21.

3.

Giants in the Land

1 Samuel 17

"Behold, I am the LORD, the God of all flesh; is anything too difficult for Me?"—Jeremiah 32:27

We live in a land of giants. As I look at the world in which we live, I am overwhelmed with the enormity of the problems facing our society: homelessness, starvation, poverty, over-crowding, air and water pollution, toxic waste disposal, drug and alcohol abuse, a deteriorating legal system, an enormous national debt, violence and crime. On a personal level, there are people who are giants, if not in size, then in their impact on our daily or future existence. Relationships with spouses or ex-spouses, children, parents, in-laws, employers, employees, students, teachers, or professors can overwhelm our spirits. Circumstances such as health, financial, or career status may loom large. Character traits including our habits, attitudes, personality foibles, or emotional struggles and addictions can present overwhelming obstacles to personal development and progress.

While the giants we face today are different in appearance from the giants living in Canaan from the time of Joshua to

David, their impact has changed very little. We can learn something
of how to deal with our spiritual giants by examining the encounter
between David and the giant Goliath. The popular Sunday school story is found in 1 Samuel 17, and begins as follows:

The Philistines gathered their armies for battle; and they were
gathered at Socoh which belongs to Judah. (1 Samuel 17:1)

In other words, the Philistines were trespassers on land that belonged to Judah. They had no right to be where they were.

Saul and the men of Israel were gathered, and camped in the val-
ley of Elah, and drew up in battle array to encounter the Philistines.
And the Philistines stood on the mountain on one side while Israel
stood on the mountain on the other side, with the valley between them.
(1 Samuel 17:2–3)

The battle was stalemated. No progress was being made by the Israelites in ridding their country of this enemy. Every morning when
they awoke they were immediately faced with this problem, and they
were getting nowhere fast.

A champion came out from the armies of the Philistines named
Goliath, from Gath, whose height was six cubits and a span. And he
had a bronze helmet on his head, and he was clothed with scale armor
which weighed five thousand shekels of bronze. He also had bronze
greaves on his legs and a bronze javelin slung between his shoulders.
And the shaft of his spear was like a weaver's beam, and the head of
his spear weighed six hundred shekels of iron; his shield-carrier also
walked before him. (1 Samuel 17:4–7)

Goliath's reputation preceded him, as he was known as a champion, a winner, the kind of person who is always chosen first in pickup
basketball games. He was incredibly tall, about 9' 9", which by today's

standards is behemoth. He was not the only big person alive, as there were other giants living in Gath at the time (2 Samuel 21:20–22). Giants had lived in the land for a number of years, but by the time of Joshua, they had been confined to Gaza, Gath, and Ashdod (Joshua 11:22).

This man was heavily armed. One hundred shekels is about a kilogram, so 5000 shekels is about 50 kilograms or 110 pounds. His spearhead alone weighed about fifteen pounds, and this was carried at the end of a large wooden beam. In all he carried about two hundred pounds of armor and weapons. This was a very strong man, and his protection was seemingly impenetrable.

He stood and shouted to the ranks of Israel, and said to them, "Why do you come out to draw up in battle array? Am I not the Philistine and you servants of Saul? Choose a man for yourselves and let him come down to me. If he is able to fight with me and kill me, then we will become your servants; but if I prevail against him and kill him, then you shall become our servants." (1 Samuel 17:8–9)

The entire focus of the battle had shifted to Goliath. All eyes were on him and everything else seemed secondary. It was impossible to think about or devote any time or energy to other issues.

This same thing had happened before when the twelve spies went into Canaan to report back to Moses. In their report they recounted

"All the people whom we saw in it are men of great size." (Numbers 13:32)

Theirs was a false statement, because in the preceding verses of Numbers 13 the spies reported seeing a variety of people, only some of whom were giants. The fact that there were some giants was enough to distort their view and make them focus solely on this one group of people.

Again the Philistine said, "I defy the ranks of Israel this day; give me a man that we may fight together." When Saul and all Israel heard these words of the Philistines, they were dismayed and greatly afraid. (1 Samuel 17:10–11)

The presence of the giant robbed the men of Israel of their masculinity. Goliath asked for a man, but no one came forward, indicating that none of them, not even Saul, felt that they could measure up to Goliath's definition of manhood. This is noteworthy because one of the reasons Saul was chosen to be king of Israel was because of his manly stature; he stood head and shoulders above his compatriots (1 Samuel 9:2).

The pressure on the Israelites was relentless. This threatening activity went on for forty days (1 Samuel 17:16). During this time, there was plenty of feinting and verbal sparring and shouting of war cries (1 Samuel 17:20), but there was no engagement of the enemy. The Israelites did not have an effective battle plan, and they were at a complete standstill.

So it is with us when we are faced with spiritual giants. The spiritual giants that we face are trespassers and intruders. Our rights as Christians are violated by the appearance of these giants. God has promised Christians a victorious life, so that conflicts with spiritual giants that intrude into our life should be short-lived. It is God's desire to quickly run these giants out of our lives.

Giants always seem like winners, having every possible advantage, and being heavily armed against attack, they seem indestructible. They usually have a strong foothold, having been around for some time, and do not appear to be easily dislodged. A giant gets the full focus of our attention. We lose sleep and cannot concentrate on other matters at hand because the giant is always there, taunting and pressuring us. Giants rob us of our manhood or womanhood, making us feel insignificant and totally incapable of making progress. Perhaps you feel inadequate as a parent or a spouse, a disciplinarian, decision maker, bread winner, or lover. We get no respect from giants.

Giants bring our Christian growth to a standstill. Perhaps there is religious activity, including regular church attendance, but it amounts to little more than ineffectual feinting and sparring, with no battle plan, and no substantial engagement of the enemy. Reading through the Bible in a year or reading motivational books with twelve easy steps to success seem not to address the specific problem we face. We are left frustrated, not knowing what to try next.

I faced my biggest personal giant during my second year of graduate study. It is during this period that five faculty members administer a three-hour oral examination, the results of which are monumental. If you pass this examination, you qualify to continue study and will, in all likelihood, receive a Ph.D. degree. If you fail this exam, you are finished with graduate school and must try to get a real job.

It is not an overstatement to say that I was totally consumed by anxiety before this exam. I studied in preparation for this exam continuously for six months. During this time, my wife saw only the back of my head. We had little social life, and church activity was kept to a minimum.

It is a trivial matter for any five people to find something that one nervous student does not know. Within five minutes of the beginning of the exam (it seemed), my examiners whizzed through everything that I knew and found the borders of my knowledge, where they camped for the rest of the time. I was emotionally devastated by the revelation of how little I knew, and how easy it was for others to expose my ignorance. I remember the words of my advisor as he later announced the results of the exam. "Jim, you did not do as well as we had hoped, but the committee has decided to pass you anyway." In other words, I had failed the exam, but he had argued for me and had convinced the committee to be lenient and give me a chance, one that I had not earned, to continue my studies anyway.

For the next three months, the personal shock and disappointment of failure weighed heavily on me. I was mentally and spiritually exhausted, unable to study or function as a normal student. I went through all the obvious arguments trying to convince myself that

things were not so bad (after all, I had passed, hadn't I?), but no argument succeeded in restoring my self-confidence and motivation.
The most demanding intellectual activity I could handle was to
record the scores from game after game of Solitaire. In other words,
I experienced all the symptoms that come from being attacked by a
giant.

When David showed up at Socoh, he had no idea what was happening on the battlefield. He had been sent there by his father to deliver some provisions and to check on his three oldest brothers, who
had followed Saul into battle. When he arrived at the Israelite camp,
he got no respect. On seeing Goliath, he asked a simple, but pointed,
question:

*David spoke to the men who were standing by him, saying, "What
will be done for the man who kills this Philistine, and takes away the
reproach from Israel? For who is this uncircumcised Philistine, that
he should taunt the armies of the living God?"* (1 Samuel 17:26)

David's oldest brother, Eliab, did not have much regard for David
and chastised him with angry words.

*Eliab his oldest brother heard when he spoke to the men; and Eli-
ab's anger burned against David and he said, "Why have you come
down? And with whom have you left those few sheep in the wilderness? I know your insolence and the wickedness of your heart; for you
have come down in order to see the battle."* (1 Samuel 17:28)

Eliab accused David of being an irresponsible little kid, driven by
boyish curiosity, like a firetruck chaser, who was up to no good, and
who could only get in the way. David's response shows his exaspera-
tion and frustration at being continually treated like a little child.

"What have I done this time? I just asked a question!" (1 Samuel
17:29, my paraphrase)

David kept asking various people about what was being done with Goliath, and eventually King Saul heard about David and sent for him. As soon as he came before Saul, David volunteered to fight Goliath.

David said to Saul, "Let no man's heart fail on account of him; your servant will go and fight with this Philistine." (1 Samuel 17:32)

Saul was direct in his response to David.

Saul said to David, "You are not able to go against this Philistine to fight with him; for you are but a youth while he has been a warrior from his youth." (1 Samuel 17:33)

In other words, Saul had decided that because of his youth and apparent inexperience, David was not man enough to fight Goliath. I am not sure how Saul knew what was needed since he himself did not have whatever it was.

I wonder if this is the treatment we give the giant-slayers around us. It is so easy to become resigned to living with giants. When someone comes along with the attitude that "enough is enough" and it is time to rid ourselves of this burden, we disdain them and are threatened by them. We criticize them or ignore them as not really knowing the situation, or not being able to do any better than our own failed efforts, using excuses like, "This is the way it has always been" or, "What else can you expect from an imperfect person?" It can often happen that new Christians with tremendous zeal and vitality are squelched in their enthusiasm because "that's not the way we do things around here," or because "the problem is much bigger than you understand."

David was not discouraged by the naysayers. Rather, he was sustained by three facts. First, he had a different *perception of the situation.* David saw that Goliath was challenging and taunting the armies of the living God, and in David's mind, this was intolerable. It is understandable that Goliath could hold off an ordinary army, but not God's army.

When we look at a situation, we often do not see the full picture. David would tell us that we do not comprehend the incredible strength of the living God. A similar situation occurred with Elisha and his servant when they were surrounded by an army led by the king of Aram.

When the attendant of the man of God had risen early and gone out, behold, an army with horses and chariots was circling the city. And his servant said to him, "Alas, my master! What shall we do?" (2 Kings 6:15)

It is natural to panic if we sense that we are alone and surrounded by the enemy. But panic is replaced with confidence when we understand the awesome power of the living God.

He answered, "Do not fear, for those who are with us are more than those who are with them." Then Elisha prayed and said, "O, LORD, I pray, open his eyes that he may see." And the LORD opened the servant's eyes, and he saw; and behold, the mountain was full of horses and chariots of fire all around Elisha. (2 Kings 6:16–17)

The problem, of course, was with the servant's perception. When his eyes were opened, the servant saw that he and Elijah were surrounded by the army of God and their confidence soared. So also for us, our perception is distorted and we need to see that God's strength is greater than the strength of any giant we may face. God is more than man enough to face Goliath.

Greater is He who is in you than he who is in the world. (1 John 4:4)

The second fact behind David's confidence was his realization that *God had been training him for this event.* David recognized that God had used different events in his sheep-herding days in the wilderness to prepare him for this one. He had killed both a lion and a bear in order to protect his sheep. In other words, David recognized that God had been disciplining him and training him while he was tending sheep, and if this giant were the next situation with which he was confronted, then his training must be adequate, because God would not put him into a situation for which he was not prepared (1 Corinthians 10:13).

You do not expect a person to step to the plate in the ninth inning of the last game of the World Series and hit the game-winning home run, as did Joe Carter in the 1993 World Series, if he has not put in long hours of physical and mental training before the event. David's training included not only the physical discipline of watching for and killing wild animals, but also the spiritual disciplines, like prayer and meditation, worship, and service. You see, what one does under pressure is, to a large measure, the natural outflow of the life lived when not on the spot. A successful performance at the moment of crisis rests essentially on the depths of wise and rigorous preparation.

David's training to fight giants came while he was tending sheep. The analogy for us is that our training to fight giants comes mostly in the quiet moments of life, in prayer, meditation, service, or worship. The seemingly menial tasks of shepherding, like serving breakfast at the rescue mission, driving the church van to the youth retreat, babysitting the small children of a struggling young family, leading a devotional for a group of friends, or writing songs of praise to God, are all acts through which God trains us to fight the giants of life.

The spiritual disciplines are not optional, but neither are they onerous. I think that prayer and meditation have a bad reputation because of some misconceptions we have about them. To meditate means to ponder, to muse, or to ruminate over. In the Old Testament, meditation also included the idea of having a silent conversation with oneself, and one might even be seen moving his lips or uttering some low, indecipherable sounds. Prayer is simply including God in the conversation.

Prayer and meditation do not require that you live a monastic existence. They do not require long periods of unbroken silence, or total solitude, although you do need to take advantage of those lulls in your day that are available. David spoke of meditating in his bed at night, or during the night watch (Psalm 63:6). A friend of mine uses his time riding the bus to and from work in prayer and meditation, while a homemaker I know looks forward to folding laundry for the same reason. You also do not have to be a Bible scholar or theologian to spend meaningful time in prayer and meditation. You simply need to bring God and His Word into the ordinary pattern of your thought life.

Even Jesus had to be trained to prepare Him for the difficulties He had to face. Being the Son of God did not relieve Him of the necessity of a life of preparation, of disciplines, lived outside of the public eye.

Although He was a Son, He learned obedience from the things which He suffered. (Hebrews 5:8)

The third fact of David's confidence was his *refusal to fight by expected methods.* David did not try to fight power with power, or flesh with flesh. He would not fight by the rules that Goliath was trying to establish. He was not willing to wear Saul's armor or use Saul's sword. Saul, the man of flesh, could not understand this refusal, and he viewed David as unprotected. But David knew that the outcome of the battle was not within his own control anyway. The outcome of the battle was to be determined by God.

David said to the Philistine, "You come to me with a sword, a spear, and a javelin [symbols of physical power], *but I come to you in the name of the LORD of hosts, the God of the armies of Israel, whom you have taunted. This day the LORD will deliver you up into my hands . . . . that all the earth may know that there is a God in Israel, and that all this assembly may know that the LORD does not deliver by sword or by spear; for the battle is the LORD's and He will give you into our hands."* (1 Samuel 17:45–47)

Swords, spears, and javelins are not symbols of power in today's world, but it does not take much looking around to find out what some of them are. Paging through an airline magazine I recently came across an advertisement proclaiming, "In business, you don't get what you deserve, you get what you negotiate." The text of the advertisement was an encouragement to sign up for a seminar on effective negotiating, so that "you can get what you want by negotiating better deals."

Is that true? In order to get a fair salary or salary increase, must I set up a meeting with my boss to tell him of my special accomplishments? To get a good pay raise, must I look for another job in order to establish my market value and then hope for an attractive counteroffer? If I choose not to pursue this tactic, will I be exploited monetarily? And what should I do when (not *if*, but *when*!) a colleague with less seniority and experience receives a salary that is substantially higher than mine, or when I do not receive all the recognition that I obviously deserve?

In contrast to "power negotiators," David knew that success in fighting Goliath did not depend on the brandishing of his own strengths; the battle belonged to the Lord.

It happened when the Philistine rose and came and drew near to meet David, that David ran quickly toward the battle line to meet the Philistine. And David put his hand into his bag and took from it a stone and slung it, and struck the Philistine on his forehead. And the stone sank into his forehead, so that he fell on his face to the ground. (1 Samuel 17:48–49)

Because David refused to measure Goliath with the yardstick of physical power, he noticed a unique vulnerability of giants that all other military strategists failed to see. The huge size and physical power of Goliath had blinded the army of Israel to the fact that large men are often clumsy and slow. As is sometimes said of huge basketball players, he can't jump, but he's slow. Goliath's armament was designed to protect against large, slow-moving objects. A single large javelin is relatively easy to deflect. But a heavy shield is of no use against a small stone traveling at over a hundred miles an hour, and a clumsy giant is too slow afoot to keep track of a swift-footed youth. Goliath had the wrong defense for David's offense, and Goliath, not David, was vulnerable and unprotected.

Joshua saw the same feature of the giants in Canaan when he told the nation of Israel,

"Do not fear the people of the land, for they shall be our prey. Their protection has been removed from them, and the LORD is with us; do not fear them." (Numbers 14:9)

Our protection is never based on our own strength. For our every strength, there are perhaps dozens of weaknesses that make us vulnerable to attack from the enemy. No intelligent enemy attacks directly against an area of strength, but against an area of weakness. So too with giants, there is always an area of weakness and vulnerability, and an offense against which their defense is inadequate. As long as we view the giant the way he wants to be viewed, we will be overwhelmed, defenseless, and stalemated. When we come to see that the battle is the Lord's, and that it is not fought using weapons of power or flesh, the giants are exposed and defenseless.

This battle was won when David viewed Goliath from God's perspective, allowing God to give David the idea to use a sling-propelled stone, against which Goliath had no defense. That was creative thinking.

I have come to believe that creativity, that is, the thinking of a good new idea, is a miracle. Creativity does not occur as the consequence of the natural world or as the result of natural, deterministic, physical processes. Creativity is not governed by the laws of nature; Nature is reproductive, but not creative. Thomas Edison was only partly correct when he said that genius is one percent inspiration and ninety-nine percent perspiration. No amount of perspiration will guarantee any inspiration. As badly as I want a good idea or as hard as I work to get a good idea, there is nothing I can do to become inspired.

In that sense, inspiration, the thinking of a good idea, is a supernatural event, a miracle. To be sure, creativity can be stifled or suppressed, and Jesus preceded Edison with the realization that what we do with one insightful idea (how much perspiration we apply) determines if we will be given more (Mark 4:24–25).

The real battle is always a battle for the mind and the spirit. The battle with Goliath was won by David when he allowed God to influence his mind, and God gave David good ideas. Jesus stated repeatedly (in John 14:10, for instance) that God initiated everything He did. The New Testament writers called this being indwelt by God's Spirit, allowing His Spirit to influence our thought processes, and not being confused or misled by the natural reactions of our lower nature.

We will have victory over the giants in our lives when we think about giants in the same way as did David. We need to realize that the giant is taunting the armies of the living God, of which we are members, and that

1) since God does not look up to giants, neither should we.

We need to recognize,

2) that God has used our experiences in the past to prepare us for this event,

3) that the battle is the Lord's.

Finally, by refusing to fight using expected methods, as

4) we allow His Spirit to direct us,

we gain the fresh perspective and ideas needed to expose the weaknesses of the giant and render him defenseless,

"Not by might nor by power, but by My Spirit," says the LORD *of hosts.* (Zechariah 4:6)

Study Guide for Chapter 3

1. For content:
• Read 1 Samuel 17.

• Why was David so confident when all the odds seemed to be stacked against him?

2. For further study:
• What do Proverbs 3:26 and Proverbs 14:26 teach about confidence?

• What was the "giant" that the apostle Peter faced in Acts 4 (see verses 18 and 21)? Even though he was uneducated and untrained, Peter had a confidence that was noticed and recognized by others. What was the source of his confidence (verse 13; see also verse 29)?

• One command is given three times in Joshua 1:6–9. How does meditation on God's Word help us to heed the command?

• Meditation on God's Word helps us stand up to what "giants" mentioned in Psalm 1:1–2?

• What was the source of initiative in Jesus' life? (cf. John 5:30; 8:28, 42; 12:29; 14:10)

* List some of the benefits of meditating on God's Word mentioned in Psalm 119.

3. For application:
• Identify some giants that you currently face.

• Does lack of confidence in God affect what you say to other people about your beliefs? How would you answer Isaiah 57:11?

• How are you using the quiet moments of life to prepare yourself to face your giants?

• How is your outlook on life influenced by the things that your mind dwells on? How does the encouragement of the apostle Paul in Philippians 4:8 relate to this?

4. For action:
* Read the biography of William Wilberforce. See, for example, Garth Lean's *God's Politician: William Wilberforce's Struggle.* (London: Darton, Longman, and Todd, 1980), or John Pollock's *William Wilberforce* (New York: St. Martin's Press, 1978).

5. For personal commitment:
3-by-5: Memorize 1 Samuel 17:47.

4.

I Just Don't Feel Like Singing

2 Chronicles 20

I could do without Mondays. My weekends are always very full. On Saturdays I put the finishing touches on my Sunday school lesson, do some chores around the house, run some errands, drive the family taxi for my teenage children and their friends, and if there is time, do some skiing, hiking, or biking with my son. Sunday is filled with church and Sunday school class, followed by an afternoon of various family activities, so that by Sunday evening I am exhausted and ready for a rest. Monday always comes about one day too soon.

The inscription on the coffee cup says it well: "The day sure seems long when I get to work on time." So why is it that Monday morning is also the time when unforeseen difficulties seem to pile up, one after another? If there is ever a day that I need to let God fight my battles for me, it is Monday. The problem is that too often I am not sure I know how that works.

I know that I am not alone. Many Christians would be happy to let God fight their battles for them, but they're not sure what that entails. What exactly do I have to do? Is there a waiting list somewhere on which to sign up? Is there a special emergency phone number I need to know for when things get really bad? Does God carry a pager?

We learn something about how to prepare for battle from the experience of Jehoshaphat.

It came about after this that the sons of Moab and the sons of Ammon, together with some of the Meunites, came to make war against Jehoshaphat. Then some came and reported to Jehoshaphat, saying, "A great multitude is coming against you from beyond the sea, out of Edom and behold, they are in Hazazon-tamar. (2 Chronicles 20:1–2)

Judah's enemies were attacking, and there was no place to run. To the north, the nation of Israel had recently been defeated by the king of Aram (Syria), and the Ammonites and Moabites were coming from the east. To make things worse, the Edomites were coming from the region of Mt. Seir to the south. Jehoshaphat was surrounded with no place to run, and he was afraid. What should he do? What could he do?

This particular group of attackers had a unique history. Unlike the inhabitants of Canaan, who were dreadfully wicked and whose destruction was deserved, the Edomites and Moabites were "friends" or distant relatives. Edomites were descendants of Esau, and the Moabites and Ammonites were descendants of Lot, to whom God had given land southeast of Canaan. As the nation of Israel was making the long wilderness trek from Egypt to Canaan, the Israelites had been instructed not to harm Edom or Moab, and now, here they were, ready to attack king Jehoshaphat and Judah.

And Jehoshaphat was afraid and turned his attention to seek the LORD; *and proclaimed a fast throughout all Judah.* (2 Chronicles 20:3)

Jehoshaphat did not know what else to do, so he did the only thing that he could think of that made sense. He declared a fast and started to pray. That's not a bad start. In fact, a good way to prepare for your daily battles is to start every day with prayer.

Let's look at what Jehoshaphat said in his prayer:

"O LORD, the God of our fathers, art Thou not God in the heavens? And art Thou not ruler over all the kingdoms of the nations? Power and might are in Thy hand so that no one can stand against Thee." (2 Chronicles 20:6)

Jehoshaphat began his prayer acknowledging that God alone is ruler of all heaven and earth, and that there is no nation that can stand up to Him. God was not surprised or frightened by this situation, not even a little bit, nor was He uncertain about the outcome.

"Didst Thou not, O our God, drive out the inhabitants of this land before Thy people Israel, and give it to the descendants of Abraham Thy friend forever?" (2 Chronicles 20:7)

Jehoshaphat gave a quick review of their history, reminding himself and the people of God's promise of the past, and His faithfulness to that promise.

They lived in it, and have built Thee a sanctuary there for Thy name, saying, 'Should evil come upon us, the sword, or judgment, or pestilence, or famine, we will stand before this house and before Thee (for Thy name is in this house) and cry to Thee in our distress, and Thou wilt hear and deliver us.' " (2 Chronicles 20:8–9)

Regardless of what happened to them, Jehoshaphat affirmed that his dependence was on God, to stand before Him in their weakness and distress. They had nowhere else to turn.

"Now behold, the sons of Ammon and Moab and Mount Seir, whom Thou didst not let Israel invade when they came out of the land of Egypt (they turned aside from them and did not destroy them), behold how they are rewarding us, by coming to drive us out from Thy possession which Thou hast given us as an inheritance." (2 Chronicles 20:10–11)

Jehoshaphat showed his frustration. "It's not fair! We were kind enough (or dumb enough!) to let them alone when we passed by them on the way to Canaan, and now, here they are, trying to take our land away from us. We kept our part of the bargain and look at how they treat us now that they have the advantage."

"O our God, wilt Thou not judge them? For we are powerless before this great multitude who are coming against us; nor do we know what to do, but our eyes are on Thee." (2 Chronicles 20:12)

Jehoshaphat's prayer was a good summary of the situation. Here is my paraphrase of the prayer: "God, You alone are all-powerful. You are the One who fought for us in the past, and we have come to rely solely on You. We are getting a bad deal from our enemies. We could have wiped them out years ago and did not because You told us not to. Now that they are stronger, there is nothing we can do to divert them, so we throw ourselves at Your mercy to take care of us."

Usually we do not come to this position of relying on God so quickly. Instead, we have to learn from our numerous mistakes that the other things we rely upon are inadequate.

Recall that when he ordered the census, David made the mistake of thinking that large numbers would secure his future. We fall into a similar trap when we assume that belonging to a large church in a large denomination or to political activity groups will give us the clout we need to prevail, or that working for a large company will give us the financial security we desire.

Or, perhaps we try to overpower the enemy, using high pressure tactics, like nagging, or angry picketing.

"Cursed is the man who trusts in mankind and makes flesh his strength, and whose heart turns away from the LORD." (Jeremiah 17:5)

Sometimes we rely on treaties, alliances and compromises to smooth things out. King Asa made a serious mistake when he made a treaty with the king of Aram to defeat Baasha, king of Israel. Later, King Jehoshaphat, hoping to make peace with Ahab and Jezebel, arranged for his son Jehoram to marry their daughter Athaliah. But compromises with the enemy are doomed to failure and often lead to even worse trouble than they solve. God wants us to remain separate, unencumbered, and strong.

The eyes of the LORD move to and fro throughout the earth that He may strongly support those whose heart is completely His. You [Asa] have acted foolishly in this. Indeed, from now on you will surely have wars. (2 Chronicles 16:9)

Perhaps we depend on our friends, neighbors, or relatives to help us get through a tough situation. The prophet Isaiah describes how people often try to encourage each other to stick to a difficult task.

"The coastlands have seen and are afraid; the ends of the earth tremble; they have drawn near and have come. Each one helps his neighbor, and says to his brother, 'Be strong!' So the craftsman encourages the smelter, and he who smooths metal with the hammer encourages him who beats the anvil, saying of the soldering, 'It is good'; and he fastens it with nails, that it should not totter." (Isaiah 41:5–7)

Do you catch what Isaiah is saying? He is being sarcastic here, pointing out that people "pump each other up" to construct things (idols) that cannot stand on their own two feet without tottering. But God, through Isaiah, says that we should not look around us to see if we have compatriots to push us on, or if we are part of a popular movement, but rather we should rely on God alone. As Christians, we work actively to clean up the environment or promote family values, not because it is the popular or politically correct thing to do, but in response to God's motivating and strengthening us to fight these battles.

"You whom I have taken from the ends of the earth, and called from its remotest parts, and said to you, 'You are my servant, I have

chosen you and not rejected you. Do not fear, for I am with you; do not look anxiously about you, for I am your God. I will strengthen you, surely I will help you, surely I will uphold you with My righteous right hand.' " (Isaiah 41:9–10)

When God gives His people a battle to fight, He does not expect the secular world to support us. Instead, He expects us to rely on Him.

Jehoshaphat finished his prayer and the people were standing there, wondering what to do next, a priest named Jahaziel was moved by the Spirit of God to stand up and speak.

"Listen, all Judah and the inhabitants of Jerusalem and King Jehoshaphat: thus says the LORD to you, 'Do not fear or be dismayed because of this great multitude, for the battle is not yours but God's' " (2 Chronicles 20:15)

It is significant that this speech was given by a priest, not by an officer of the army. When God fought a battle, the priest was to give the speech of encouragement, and not the officers. Remarkably, the officer's primary task was to send home those people who were not mentally and spiritually prepared for war. The sequence of events in preparing for battle were delineated by Moses.

"When you go out to battle against your enemies and see horses and chariots and people more numerous than you, do not be afraid of them; for the LORD your God, who brought you up from the land of Egypt, is with you. Now it shall come about that when you are approaching the battle, the priest shall come near and speak to the people. And he shall say to them, 'Hear, O Israel, you are approaching the battle against your enemies today. Do not be fainthearted. Do not be afraid, or panic, or tremble before them, for the LORD your God is the one who goes with you, to fight for you against your enemies, to save you.' " (Deuteronomy 20:1–4)

Now here is an interesting question. Why is it that this motivational speech was to be given by the priest and not by the officers of the army?

The answer lies in the nature of the speech. The speech that a general gives is to build up the soldiers' morale and to convince them that their training, abilities, and equipment are superior to those of the enemy, and that they can win if they are determined enough. Who can forget the rousing speech given by George C. Scott, acting as General Patton, in which he said, "The purpose of war is not to die for your country. The purpose of war is to make the other guy die for his!"

The speech given by the priest is different. His purpose is to convince us that God will fight for us. The team that has God on its side will certainly win, and we want to know if God is on our side or not. Because he acts as a mediator between God and men, the priest has special insight into this determination. Jahaziel's name means "Jehovah reveals," and that is exactly what God did through Jahaziel.

How can I be assured that God is on my side and not on the side of the other guy? The problem is that God is a holy God and will not tolerate sin and will not fight for us if we are not clean before Him.

Remember what God told Joshua after Israel was defeated at Ai.

"There are things under the ban in your midst, O Israel. You cannot stand before your enemies until you have removed the things from under the ban in your midst." (Joshua 7:13b)

In other words, as long as there is sin in your life, God will not fight your battles for you; you stand alone, but alone you cannot stand. The priest cannot proclaim reassuring words of God's support until he first issues the command for repentance.

"Rise up! Consecrate the people and say, 'Consecrate yourselves for tomorrow.'" (Joshua 7:13a)

The real issue that you face before the battle is, "Are you clean before God?" not, "Are you strong and powerful?" Here is where the battle is won or lost! Becoming clean is difficult. Like Dennis the Menace, we don't want to admit we are dirty. Becoming clean before God is unpleasant because it involves standing before a righteous God, taking a hard and honest look at ourselves and coming to realize how unworthy we are, and then confessing our sin to God. I fear that we view cleanliness much like I did when I was a young boy; we take a bath (or read a confessional prayer at church) once a week whether we need it or not.

Cleanliness before God is absolutely crucial; you cannot stand before your enemies if there is sin resident in your life. You will never have victory over lust or greed or depression if you keep pandering yourself with your leisure time choices. You must consecrate yourself, that is, set yourself apart from negative, sinful influences, and dedicate yourself to living clean before God.

After Jahaziel had revealed to Jehoshaphat that God was on his side, he instructed the people on what they had to do next.

" 'Tomorrow go down against them. Behold, they will come up by the ascent of Ziz, and you will find them at the end of the valley in front of the wilderness of Jeruel. You need not fight in this battle; station yourselves, stand and see the salvation of the LORD on your behalf, O Judah and Jerusalem.' Do not fear or be dismayed; tomorrow go out to face them, for the LORD is with you." (2 Chronicles 20:16–17)

If I had been the author of 2 Chronicles, I probably would have omitted this part of the story. I am not a confrontational person and much prefer to avoid conflict. When involved in a confrontational discussion, I become flustered and flushed, cannot think or communicate clearly, nor argue convincingly. For me, as for Mark Twain, repartee is what I realize I should have said twenty-four hours too late. When trying to find ways to handle a difficulty, I like the idea of writing an anonymous letter. I could easily have been the author of the quote:

A man is not a man until people know exactly what he thinks.
—Anonymous

The message of this passage to me is simple: "Jim, you must confront the situation head-on. You cannot hide, hoping it will go away on its own, but you must calmly and directly address the problem to see how God will make the argument, and fight the battle.

For other less cowardly people, there is a different message. It may be that you love a good fight, and are ready to jump into the fray at a moment's notice. For you, the message is to not charge ahead, with guns blazing, in full attack of the problem. This would be the easy way out for you. For you, the message is to stand and be quiet and let God deliver. God does not expect you to win the argument; He wants to do that for you. Your job is to stand and watch while He fights the battle.

The morning following the message from Jahaziel to Jehoshaphat, everyone got up early in the morning to go out to meet the enemy. On their way out to the wilderness of Tekoa, Jehoshaphat gave a strange order.

[Jehoshaphat] *appointed those who sang to the Lord and those who praised Him in holy attire, as they went out before the army and said, "Give thanks to the Lord, for His lovingkindness is everlasting."* (2 Chronicles 20:21)

Jehoshaphat directed the choir members, all dressed up in their choir robes, to go in front of the army in the direction of the enemy. He also gave them the words (and maybe even the music) to the song they were to sing. I imagine that being in the choir that morning was not as desirable as on other occasions. It is okay to be in the choir when one can be seen up front leading a worship service, but to lead the army into battle is not what they had signed up for. They didn't think this is what the recruiting officer meant when he said they would "be all that you can be." On mornings like this, I just don't feel like singing. Maybe it would be better to stay home.

But a remarkable thing happened on the way to the front lines.

When they began singing and praising, the LORD set ambushes against the sons of Ammon, Moab, and Mount Seir, who had come

*against Judah; so they were routed. For the sons of Ammon and Moab
rose up against the inhabitants of Mount Seir destroying them completely, and when they had finished with the inhabitants of Seir, they
helped to destroy one another.* (2 Chronicles 20:22–23)

Notice the wording here. The enemy self-destructed *after*, not before, the singers started singing and praising God. I imagine the scene
was not unlike the scene from the *Sound of Music* in which the von
Trapp children tried to cheer themselves by singing "My Favorite
Things." The song itself was not enough to lift their spirits, but when
they were joined by the returning Maria, their singing became vibrant
and alive and full of emotion. So too I imagine Jehoshaphat's choir
sang with uncertainty at first, but as their song progressed and they began to understand that their Father was with them, their singing became confident, boisterous, and vivacious.

Worship has this effect on all of us. We may start out feeling low,
or depressed, or frustrated, but if we will start singing praises to God,
soon our depression or frustration is replaced with joy and thanksgiv-
ing as we recognize the presence and awesome power of God.

Singing is more than a psychological trick to boost our emotions.
It is true that music can soothe the beast in us and help us control our
moods. David played the harp for Saul to calm his maniacal tirades.
Perhaps you know the phrase from the song "Whistle a Happy Tune,"
which says, "The result of this deception is very plain to tell; for when
I fool the people I fear, I fool myself as well." But music sung in praise
to God is good theology that goes beyond psychology. Jesus said that
because God is Spirit, those who worship Him must worship in spirit
and truth. This means that we need to get our facts about God correct
(worship in truth), and we must also allow those facts to move our
spirits, that is, our emotions. I have found that when I genuinely worship in truth, by allowing the truth of God and His Word to penetrate
deeply, I cannot help but respond in spirit. A person who is not emotionally moved by God has not experienced true worship. Singing
helps us worship God when we allow the music to affect our emotions.

We break out in laughter or tears or applause because God has moved our spirits through music that praises Him.

Recently I had the opportunity to spend a day hiking on Ben Lomond in the Highlands of Scotland. The weather forecast called for scattered showers, but little did I know that they would be scattered in exactly the places I planned to be. I was underdressed for the occasion, and as I trudged up the mountain, the weather turned foul. At the top the wind was howling at about forty miles an hour, blowing sleet and snow horizontally across the ridge. My windward side was caked with ice and snow, and the switchbacks created a "rotisserie effect," so that no part of my body missed out on the experience. The hiking path alternated between rivulet and bog, making walking a challenge. I spent only a few minutes at the top, because the visibility extended no more than twenty feet.

As I turned to start down the mountain, I decided to sing, but not because I was feeling all warm and fuzzy about God. Far from it! I started to sing:

"Our God is an awesome God, He reigns from heaven above with wisdom, power, and love, our God is an awesome God."

Singing a song like this is somewhat like eating a potato chip; you can't sing it just once. The cadence of the song kept me moving at a good pace, and the song stuck in my head the whole way down the mountain. As I came off the peak, the clouds lifted for a brief moment and the sun peeked through a small break in the clouds. I looked out over beautiful, shimmering Loch Lomond, surrounded by cloud-enshrouded mountains. What a glorious sight!

When I got to my car, I was soaked to the bone, my arms and hands were so numbed with cold that I could barely manipulate the keys to open the door or start the car. My body was cold, but my spirit was full of praise for an awesome God who designed all of this beauty and who is far bigger than any of the discomfort I experienced.

So here is what we learn from Jehoshaphat about counting on God to fight our battles for us. First,

1) talk to God, in prayer and fasting, about the problem.

Reestablish your own commitment to God regardless of how He leads in the situation. Next,

2) confess your sin and make sure that you are forgiven and clean before Him.

Then,

3) be prepared to face the enemy, eyeball-to-eyeball, so that you can see how God will work things out. And finally,

4) start singing praises in worship of God.

Sing out loud and with gusto so that you can *stand and see the salvation of the Lord on your behalf.*

Study Guide for Chapter 4

1. For content:
• Read 2 Chronicles 20.

• What was Jehoshaphat's natural reaction to the difficult situation he found himself in (see 2 Chronicles 20:13)?

• What was his godly response to the situation?

2. For further study:
• The New Testament uses the word *flesh* over one hundred thirty times, yet this is not a word that is used commonly in our own daily conversation. Do a study of the word *flesh* to see what it means and how it is used. (Start with Romans 8:1–9; Galatians 5:13–24; and Philippians 3:1–4;). Can you suggest a more common phrase that expresses the same idea?

• When faced with a difficult situation, we can react naturally, following our "flesh," or we can decide to respond in a godly fashion. According to 2 Corinthians 10:5, what are we to keep under rigid control?

• According to Colossians 3:17, what actions are affected by our decision to make a godly response?

* In Judges 6–7, how many evidences can you find that Gideon was afraid?

3. For application:
• Of the four steps mentioned in this chapter for letting God fight your battles, which are the most difficult for you to do?

4. For action:
• Every morning this week, choose a "Song of the Day" to sing during quiet moments throughout the day. It may be a new chorus or a well-known selection from a familiar hymnal that emphasizes attributes of God ("Great is Thy Faithfulness," "Our God is an Awesome God," "Majesty," "He is Able").

5. For personal commitment:
3-by-5: Memorize Colossians 3:16.

5.

How To Make a Prophet

Deuteronomy 18:9–22

"Many a man proclaims his own loyalty, but who can find a trustworthy man?"—Proverbs 20:6

Dale was struggling with school. He was working for me on his Ph.D., but progress was slow and he was having a hard time maintaining his interest. He decided to take a quarter off from my research project to sort out his life and decide on his future. He was contemplating quitting school altogether.

It was then that I learned indirectly that he was having personal problems of a romantic nature. His friendship with another graduate student was becoming more serious when she decided to break off the relationship in order to date one of my colleagues. Dale took the news badly, and he had a hard time concentrating on his studies.

During the spring quarter, things seemed to improve. Dale showed more interest in his classes and expressed a desire to resume working on one of my research projects. He was to begin work early in the summer, and we discussed the project at the first of our scheduled Friday morning meetings. At that meeting, he was bleary-eyed and distracted, although he gave me assurances that he would begin work right away.

That was the last time I saw Dale. The next evening, while alone in his apartment, Dale put a gun to his head and pulled the trigger.

At times of tragedy like this, we are flooded with questions. Whose fault was this? Was there something I could have done or said? Why didn't I notice the warning signs? Why did this have to happen? The bottom line is that Dale's source of spiritual strength ran dry. He no longer had a source of strength that he could count on.

Everyone relies on some source for spiritual strength. We need physical strength to walk, or blink, or scratch an itch, and it is provided by the food we eat. We use spiritual strength to make decisions, like proposing marriage, or taking a different job, or disciplining our children. I have a student who chooses to wear a ring in his nose; his expression of uniqueness is a reflection of the fact that he has a source of spiritual strength, different from mine, perhaps, but a source of strength nonetheless.

In our society we look to many sources for spiritual strength. We draw on our families, our friends, our society. Our spiritual strength is derived from what we think is important, meaningful, and valuable, from the way we see the big picture, and ourselves fitting into that big picture. We form that picture, sometimes consciously and sometimes unconsciously, from a variety of inputs, but in all cases how we act is ultimately a reflection of our world-view. It is quite important, therefore, to consider carefully how our world-view is being shaped.

Just before his death, Moses left instructions (in Deuteronomy 17–18) with the nation of Israel on how to set up a well-structured society. His instructions included directions on how to select judges, kings, priests, and prophets. Judges were needed to maintain justice, kings were needed to maintain economic stability and a national defense, priests were needed to maintain order in the religious practices, and prophets were needed to provide "a future and a hope."

Because it is their job to shape our view of the world and to keep us focused on what is important, prophets are the most important in my view. In our society, prophets are the people who assess the trends of the future, trying to influence our decisions about careers, political and economical and social issues, life style, goals and aspirations. Right now, for example, many people in my age bracket (postwar Baby Boomers) have serious concerns about their retirement because of predictions by economists of a bankrupted Social Security system and an uncontrolled federal deficit.

Many of our most important decisions of life are guided by our prophets. When I was a senior in high school, I came under the influence of a very persuasive person who was convinced the world would end within four years—no doubt about it! In his view, I should have gone to Bible college (his, of course) for a quick year of training in evangelism and guitar-strumming, and then spent the remaining three years on the beaches of Miami for the purpose of soul-winning. There was surely no need to study mathematics or science, as there wasn't enough time left to prepare for a scientific profession.

Unfortunately, we devote very little attention to the qualifications of our prophets, and yet there are many who profess to be prophets, claiming to have special powers, knowledge of the future, or insight into life that can help a person make decisions and set goals. Some of the obvious examples of alleged prophets are Jeane Dixon, Edgar Cayce, Kahlil Gibran, Jim Jones, David Koresh, Karl Marx, Sun Myung Moon, Maharid-Ji, Ezra Taft Benson, Nostradamus, Carl Sagan, Shirley MacLaine, the Dalai Lama, and the Ayatollah Khomeini. Less apparent is the advertising industry, or the entertainment industry, with its stars and commercial endorsements, or news commentators and talk show hosts, all promoting their view of the world in the most convincing fashion possible.

To what other sources do we, in our society, look for direction? One of the primary shapers of our world-view is and has been scientific knowledge. From science we learn how the world works. We are astounded with marvels on all scales, from the submicroscopic to the astronomic. We are given speculative theories of where we came from and what is going to happen to us, yet the most we can ever learn from science is how, never why.

"Dad, were you a nerd in high school?" My daughter's question exposes the fact that many scientists are fanatically devoted to their craft. The pursuit of knowledge has for some become idolatry, bolstered by the implicit belief that here we will find answers to our quest for meaning and purpose in life. Yet, the self-proclaimed prophet of science, Carl Sagan, with his unusual blend of scientific information and Eastern mysticism, cannot help us. And Stephen Hawking concludes his book *A Brief History of Time* unable to answer the three gnawing questions: "What is the nature of the universe?" "What is our place in it and where did it and we come from?" "Why is it the way it is?"

The idea that dominates our culture today is scientific materialism. We are in the age of the "technofix," believing that we can fix any problem with technology, whether by genetic engineering, fuel efficiency, or safer condoms. The advances in computer technology, biochemistry, and medical technology and their spinoffs are truly spectacular. Surely you've noticed the amazing things surgeons can do with lasers and microsurgery these days. But as successful as all of these have been, they have been equally unsuccessful at solving our societal problems. People starve by the millions, our environment is being deliberately polluted, wars are being fought, bigotry and injustice are rampant, children are abused by their parents, and we have no sustenance for the emptiness of our souls.

Another place that people in our society turn for guidance and strength is psychology. In the sixties and seventies, it seemed that everyone had a therapist or participated in some form of sensitivity group or analysis. In the early days of our marriage, I shamelessly embarrassed my wife far too often in the misguided belief that by baring my soul, healing would take place (I now realize that I was the heel with a bared sole).

Today the emphasis on analysis and therapy has waned, but the self-improvement/self-esteem business is booming, producing over 4,000 new book titles a year, in addition to tapes, videos, and motivational seminars. Surely you have heard the foremost guiding principle proclaimed by the prophets of this belief system: "He or she just needs more self-esteem." As a society, we are addicted to the drug of individualism.

The prophet Isaiah knew that when we try to depend on ourselves as a source of spiritual strength we are sure to fail. His summary of the Me-First generation is on target.

> *"You felt secure in your wickedness and said, 'No one sees me,' your wisdom and your knowledge, they have deluded you; for you have said in your heart, 'I am, and there is no one besides me.' But evil will come on you which you will not know how to charm away; and disaster will fall on you for which you cannot atone, and destruction about which you do not know will come on you suddenly."* (Isaiah 47:10–11)

An increasingly popular source for meaning and spiritual strength in today's society is the New Age movement and the occult. There is a resurgence in animism and spiritism, evidenced by our society's fascination with the religious practices of Native Americans. Earth Day (April 22) is taking on the aura of a religious holiday, and planting trees has ritual significance. Yet, interest in fortune-telling, astrology, pyramids, crystals, Ouija boards, seances, meditation, and the like is by no means new; there is nothing new in what Shirley MacLaine writes or teaches. The New Age is indeed very old. Fascination with the occult was prevalent in biblical times, and Moses had some very strong things to say about it. In Deuteronomy, he said,

> *"There shall not be found among you anyone who makes his son or daughter pass through the fire, one who uses divination, one who practices witchcraft, or one who interprets omens, or a sorcerer, or one who casts a spell, or a medium, or a spiritist, or one who calls up the dead. For whoever does these things is detestable to the LORD."* (Deuteronomy 18:10–12a)

That should about cover it. This means that star charts, astrological signs, an emphasis on pyramids or crystals, and channeling are revolting to God. These things are disgusting and revolting to God in the same way that sodomy or sex with an animal is disgusting (Leviticus 18:24–30). We should have a better image of ourselves than to act in such disgusting ways. After all, Christians are considered by God to be holy, members of a royal family (Deuteronomy 14:1–3), and the King's kids should show a little dignity and self-respect.

Not only are these things disgusting to God, but astrology and the occult are false, based on a lie, and have no value to save. They are like the stubble of a wheat field, of no value in sustaining human life and certain to be burned off.

Stand fast now in your spells and in your many sorceries with which you have labored from your youth; perhaps you will be able to profit [make money], *perhaps you may cause trembling. You are wearied with your many counsels, let now the astrologers, those who prophecy by the stars, those who predict by the new moons, stand up and save you from what will come upon you. Behold, they have become like stubble, fire burns them; they cannot deliver themselves from the power of the flame; there will be no coal to warm by, nor a fire to sit before! So have those become to you with whom you have labored, who have trafficked with you from your youth; each has wandered in his own way. There is none to save you.* (Isaiah 47:12–15)

In fact, these things provide *absolutely no benefit whatever.*

"Behold, I am against those who prophesied false dreams," declares the LORD, "and related them, and led My people astray by their falsehoods and reckless boasting; yet I did not send them or command them, nor do they furnish this people the slightest benefit." (Jeremiah 23:32)

So the question remains for us, how are we to distinguish between true and false prophets? Are there any prophets that we should heed, and who are they? Whom can I count on to guide me in the shaping of my world-view? And how is it that I am so confident that science, psychology, New Age, and other cults are all "non-prophet" enterprises?

Fortunately for us, Moses addressed these questions in Deuteronomy 18:14–22. There he laid out criteria by which we can evaluate a person's claim to being a prophet, and decide if we should follow him or her.

"Those nations, which you shall dispossess, listen to those who practice witchcraft and to diviners, but as for you, the LORD your God has not allowed you to do so. The LORD your God will raise up for you a prophet like me from among you, from your countrymen, you shall listen to him. This is according to all that you asked of the LORD your God in Horeb on the day of the assembly, saying, 'Let me not hear again the voice of the LORD my God, let me not see this great fire anymore, lest I die.' And the LORD said to me, 'They have spoken well. I will raise up a prophet from among their countrymen like you, and I will put My words in his mouth, and he shall speak to them all that I command him. And it shall come about that whoever will not listen to My words which he shall speak in My name, I Myself will require it of him. But the prophet who shall speak a word presumptuously in My name which I have not commanded him to speak, or which he shall speak in the name of other gods, that prophet shall die.' And you may say in your heart, 'How shall we know the word which the LORD has not spoken?' When a prophet speaks in the name of the LORD, if the thing does not come about or come true, that is the thing which the LORD has not spoken. The prophet has spoken it presumptuously; you shall not be afraid of him." (Deuteronomy 18:14–22)

Moses stated that God would send at least one prophet who is worthy of our attention. First, this prophet sent by God must have the correct credentials. Twice (in verses 15 and 18) Moses said that this prophet from God will be "from your countrymen," meaning "he will be an Israelite."

Second, the prophet sent by God will have a specific style of ministry, namely he will be "like Moses" (vv. 15, 18). We get some idea of the nature of Moses' ministry from Exodus 20:18–21 (also Exodus 18:19–20). Here we see that the people were terrified to approach God, so they had Moses mediate for them. In trying to identify a prophet we should *look for someone who acts as a mediator between God and men.* A "prophet" who does not direct me toward an improved relationship with God is not worthy of my attention.

In addition, the message of Moses followed one specific theme: He *communicated the fear of God,* and at the same time *announced the possibility of peace with God.* Here we detect an important key to ascertaining any prophet of God. Jeremiah said that one thing that distinguishes the message of a true prophet from a false prophet is that the message of a true prophet has impact, because it begins by announcing that we are sinners standing in the presence of a holy God, and that peace with God comes only after repentance.

"Is not My word like fire?" declares the LORD, "and like a hammer which shatters a rock?" (Jeremiah 23:29)

Compare this with Jeremiah's words of warning (Jeremiah 23:16–22) that false prophets are those who announce that you will have peace, that all will be well and there is no need for change, when they should be turning people back from their evil ways.

"They keep saying to those who despise Me, 'The LORD has said, "You will have peace" '; and as for every one who walks in the stubbornness of his own heart, they say, 'Calamity will not come upon you.' ... But if they had stood in My council, then they would have announced My words to My people, and would have turned them back from their evil way, and from the evil of their deeds." (Jeremiah 23:17, 22)

Christ also said that the effect of His message would be that God's Spirit would convict "of sin, of righteousness, and of judgment." The person who promises peace without repentance, that things will be okay if we just adopt a positive self-image, is no prophet of God.

Biblical writings contain many other warnings about the nature of the message of a false prophet. Paul told Timothy to watch out for leaders who love to stir up controversy, whose ministry is based on being provocative and thereby attracts attention.

If anyone advocates a different doctrine, and does not agree with sound words, those of our Lord Jesus Christ, and with the doctrine conforming to godliness, he is conceited and understands nothing; but he has a morbid interest in controversial questions and disputes about words, out of which arise envy, strife, abusive language, evil suspicions, and constant friction between men of depraved mind and deprived of the truth. (1 Timothy 6:3–5)

He also warned to watch out for those who use guilt or pressure to manipulate or to obtain emotional responses, those who use the power of their personality or position to subjugate their followers.

Avoid such men as these . . . who enter into households and captivate weak women weighed down with sins [guilt], *led on by various impulses.* (2 Timothy 3:5–6)

The fourth characteristic of the true prophet is the source of his message. According to Moses (Deuteronomy 18:18) the true prophet of God is *one to whom God speaks and who says only what God wants him to say.* This means that what he says will agree with what is already known from God's Word (Deuteronomy 13:1–5; Acts 17:11). A prophet of God often brings insight, relevance, and conviction to God's Word, but never does he contradict it. On the other hand, some of the source materials for false prophets are speculation (1 Timothy 1:3–4), an overactive imagination (Jeremiah 23:16), plagiarism (Jeremiah 23:30) and dreams (Jeremiah 23:25). We can spot some of these sources when a message is nebulous with vague or speculative content, requires a specialized vocabulary, or delves into fringe areas. Specific examples are L. Ron Hubbard's Scientology,

which is full of specialized vocabulary that has little content, groups
that devote lots of attention to identifying the location of the lost tribe
of Israel, or the study of Egyptian pyramids as if they have some mys-
tical biblical significance, or cults that make continual reference to
"the gospel of Jesus Christ" without ever saying precisely what that
gospel is.

But, you might ask, how can we know if a prophet received his
message from God? Moses asked exactly the same question. His answer was succinct. If a person makes a prophecy, and the prophecy
does not come true, that person is not a true prophet and is not to be
heeded. It is pretty simple, because *a true prophet of God is one-hundred-percent accurate*. Any supposed prophet who is not one-hundred-percent accurate in his or her predictions is not a prophet from
God, and is to be ignored. End of discussion!

Furthermore, in Moses' view there was to be no second chance to
get it right; once a person was determined to be a false prophet, he was
to be stoned to death. The revelation of God's truth is serious business,
and it is to be reliably accurate. If lies are being communicated, it is
from the father of all lies, not the God of all truth. God places a high
premium on truth and has no tolerance for lies. There is no room for
experimentation or chicanery.

These then, are the criteria that enable us to determine if a person
is a prophet. A true prophet of God is one whose message

1) comes from God,

2) agrees with God's Word,

3) is about sin and the demands of a holy God for repentance,

4) has impact on people's lives,

5) discloses predictions that are one-hundred-percent accurate.

Are there any people around who meet these criteria? I think it is
quite clear that none of the alleged prophets mentioned above are true
prophets. They all fail on at least one, and in most cases, all of these
criteria.

There is one alleged prophet who deserves a closer look. In fact,
Moses promises (Deuteronomy 18:15) that God would send at least one

person who would fulfill all of these criteria. A number of other people on reading Moses' writing came to the same conclusion, namely, that Moses was predicting the arrival of at least one specific person who was a true prophet sent from God.

> *Philip found Nathanael and said to him, "We have found Him of whom Moses in the Law and also the Prophets wrote, Jesus of Nazareth, the son of Joseph."* (John 1:45)

The man we are talking about is Jesus Christ. The evidence is that Jesus satisfies all of Moses' criteria, and Jesus himself claimed that He was the one written about by Moses, and that if we believe what Moses wrote then we will certainly believe Jesus.

> *"If you believed Moses, you would believe Me; for he wrote of Me. But if you do not believe his writings, how will you believe My words?"* (John 5:46–47)

Jesus made it clear that He expected His followers to have their world-view shaped by what He taught, and to draw their spiritual strength from Him.

The point is this: Moses set out the criteria for how to evaluate a prophet. Any supposed prophet who falls short of these criteria is to be *totally ignored*. He predicted that there would be at least one person who would meet these criteria, and the evidence is that this person was Jesus Christ.

The claim of many supposed prophets is that they have some key to the future and can perhaps reveal that future to us. The claim of Jesus is different. He does not promise us knowledge of the future. Rather, He promises to those who believe in His name abundant life now and a hope for the future. In other words, He promises to give us a relationship with the God who is in control of the universe and who knows what is best for us.

These have been written that you may believe that Jesus is the Christ, the Son of God; and that believing you may have life in His name. (John 20:31)

By getting to know Jesus, I do not gain more knowledge about what will happen to me tomorrow or next week. My confidence is not the result of knowing more about the future than everyone else. I live with the same unknowns as you. Instead I am on good terms with the One who knows the past and directs the present and future, and it is this relationship with One who is totally dependable that gives me strength and hope.

"I know the plans that I have for you," declares the LORD, "plans for welfare and not for calamity to give you a future and a hope." (Jeremiah 29:11)

False gods always fail, false prophets only give false hopes, and the end of one who has no hope is despair. They do not always end their lives in such tragic fashion as did Dale, but a life without hope, lived in despair, is no less tragic.

Learning to count on God begins by establishing reliable communication with God, and this results when one is committed to following the true Prophet of God, Jesus Christ. In this relationship one discovers what really counts in life because "I know who holds the future, and I know He holds my hand."

Study Guide for Chapter 5

1. For content:
• Read Deuteronomy 18:9–22.

• In John 5:46–47, Jesus claimed to be the prophet spoken of by Moses. Specifically, what does this mean that Jesus was claiming about Himself?

• Three sources of false confidence and hope that are mentioned in the chapter are scientific knowledge, popular psychology, and New Age philosophy, but there are others. What are some other sources of false confidence in our society?

• Can you find reasons why the people on the list of so-called prophets mentioned in the chapter or the areas of confidence on your list above are disqualified from being representatives for God? Can you use this experience to spot other fraudulent people or ideas?

2. For further study:
• Make a chart comparing what Jeremiah says about false prophets (in Jeremiah 23:16–32) with the character of Jesus, by comparing the content of the following verses:
     a) Jeremiah 23:16, 32 and Mark 9:7; John 5:19
     b) Jeremiah 23:21 and Luke 4:18; John 12:49–50
     c) Jeremiah 23:22 and John 8:28–29
     d) Jeremiah 23:26 and John 5:30

• What is the common theme of Titus 1:2, Hebrews 6:18, 1 John 2:21? How does this contrast with John 8:44?

* In John 16:7–11, Jesus said that God's Spirit will convict people of three things. What are they, and why is this necessary (compare Jeremiah 23:22b)?

3. For application:
• Not all "Christian" ministries are worthy of the title. In 1 Timothy 6:3–5 (see also 1 Timothy 1:6–7) Paul warns us to avoid leaders who use certain techniques. What are they?

• What techniques does the apostle Paul warn against in 2 Timothy 3:5–7?

• How can this be applied personally? According to 2 Timothy 2:23–26, what should we avoid and what should we promote when discussing our faith with non-Christians?

4. For action:
• Be a skeptic. See how many false claims of false prophets you can identify. Use television, newspapers, magazines, and billboards to make a list identifying the messages of false prophets.

* Go to the library and look up old copies of newspapers or magazines from New Year's Day and check the accuracy of "psychics." Classify their predictions as
    a) verifiably correct
    b) verifiably wrong
    c) too nebulous to verify
    d) too general to falsify
    e) too soon to tell
What is their rate of accuracy?

5. For personal commitment:
10-by-10: Read the first ten chapters of the gospel of John, one chapter per day. Make special note of statements about truth, describing the nature of truth or the way in which truth is communicated.

PART II

Counting the Consequences

The heart is more deceitful than all else and is desperately sick; who can understand it? I, the LORD, search the heart, I test the mind, even to give to each man according to his ways, according to the results of his deeds.—Jeremiah 17:9–10

6.

Counting the Consequences of Sin

1 Samuel 11–12; Psalm 51

The news of Ervin "Magic" Johnson's announcement that he was retiring from professional basketball because he had been tested HIV-positive swept through the schools of our country faster than any recent news event I can recall. The number one question on everyone's mind was "How did he get it?" because everyone knows that the vast majority of AIDS victims are either intravenous drug users or involved with multiple sexual partners.

I found the reactions of Magic's friends and colleagues interesting. Arsenio Hall queried Magic if he could explain why bad things (like getting AIDS) can happen to good people (like Magic). Magic explained to the TV audience that he was definitely not a homosexual. He also explained that he had been naive, and didn't think this could happen to him. His former teammate, Kareem Abdul-Jabbar, said that "he wasn't cautious. His luck just ran out on him."

Magic was praised throughout the media for his courage in facing a difficult situation. Pat Riley, his former coach with the Los Angeles Lakers, said that "he is a competitor. If anyone can beat this, he can." Arsenio Hall told Magic that "we are going to beat this thing."

I have a number of questions about this situation as well. Is this another example of a bad thing happening to a good person, demonstrating once again that God is not fair? Does the fact that Magic is not homosexual justify him? Did his luck run out, and was he naive? Is it an act of courage to reveal something that cannot be hidden? Can Magic beat this thing?

Magic contracted the HIV virus through promiscuous heterosexual sex. Does the fact that Magic is rich, famous, and athletically talented make his condition more tragic than for the anonymous women from whom he got the disease or to whom he may have given it?

While the national media were climbing all over each other to find ways to glorify Magic, the biblical perspective on this situation was barely heard. The Bible, you see, says that promiscuous sex is a sin, and that the consequences of sin are both inevitable and tragic. You can count on it.

King David was a rich, famous, talented person who also fell into the trap of thinking that he could do what he wanted and get away with it without paying a substantial penalty. He was wrong.

The account of his escapade with Bathsheba is found in 2 Samuel 11–12.

It happened in the spring, at the time when kings go out to battle, that David sent Joab and his servants with him and all Israel, and they destroyed the sons of Ammon and besieged Rammah. But David stayed at Jerusalem. (2 Samuel 11:1)

David should have been at war, but instead had decided to sit this one out. By staying back in Jerusalem, he made himself vulnerable to temptation. Leisure time is a difficult time for everyone. It is during leisure time that one is more likely to get involved in unhealthy activities. I imagine that the life of a professional athlete is difficult because there is not much to do in one's hotel room while waiting for game time. On the other hand, when one is actively engaged in warfare, there is too much to think about and do to allow for distractions.

If you travel on business you know exactly what I am talking about. During the day, you are kept busy with appointments, meetings, and luncheons. In the evening there is dinner with business associates. But after dinner, or during the next day waiting for the flight home, time drags. It is then that the temptation is greatest to buy a smutty magazine from the newsstand, or view an adult movie in the privacy of your hotel room, or go out on the town looking for companionship. After all, who will know?

I keep intentionally busy when I travel. I have my portable computer or notebook at my side at all times, and at all times I keep in mind a problem to solve, an essay to write, or a lecture to prepare, so that I am anxious to get back to my room so that I can get some *real* work done. I hardly ever turn on the TV or read a newspaper; there is too much that I need to do to have time for that.

No soldier in active service entangles himself in the affairs of everyday life, so that he may please the one who enlisted him as a soldier. (2 Timothy 2:4)

Leisure activity is not all bad, and we all need periods of rest, relaxation, and recreation. But the person who stays active in ministry and is surrounded by others who are involved in Christian ministry is provided with a measure of protection against the opportunistic advances of leisure-time temptations. There is plenty of work to be done, too. You could teach a children's class, serve meals at the rescue mission, visit shut-ins or those in the hospital, lead a Bible study, take some middle schoolers on a hike, or do some yard work for an elderly person. The clear command of Scripture is to get out into the world in Christian warfare (Acts 1:8—don't remain in Jerusalem) and to stay closely involved with, and accountable to, like-minded combatants.

Yet, the problem is deeper than this.

Put on the Lord Jesus Christ, and make no provision for the flesh in regard to its lusts. (Romans 13:14)

In other words, avoid situations where the temptations are great and do not even give them an audience. Deliberately avoid situations that could be problematic. (Stay away from the newsstands in major airports.) Keeping your mind unpolluted is a battle that can be won only as you allow God's Spirit to control yours.

I say, walk by the Spirit, and you will not carry out the desire of the flesh. (Galatians 5:16)

As we have learned recently from the shocking and disappointing failures of prominent Christian leaders, keeping busy and having Christian friends is not necessarily enough protection. The only complete protection is found when we habitually and intentionally allow God's Spirit to dominate and control our own natural thought processes.

But we must understand in a practical and realistic way that *sin is opportunistic.*

When evening came David arose from his bed and walked around on the roof of the king's house, and from the roof he saw a woman bathing; and the woman was very beautiful in appearance. So David sent and inquired about the woman. And one said, "Is this not Bathsheba, the daughter of Eliam, the wife of Uriah the Hittite?" And David sent messengers and took her, and when she came to him, he lay with her; and when she had purified herself from her uncleanness, she returned to her house. (2 Samuel 11:2–4)

What was David doing in bed in the middle of the day? Perhaps he had nothing else to do so he took an afternoon nap, and as evening came could no longer sleep, so he took a stroll out on his roof. The fact that Bathsheba was taking a bath on her roof was not especially unusual. There was no indoor plumbing in those days, and baths were normally taken outdoors in enclosed courtyards. Archaeologists working at Achzib in Israel recently uncovered a statuette, dating from David's period, of a young woman sitting in an oval flat bowl, taking a bath.

So David saw this beautiful young woman taking a bath. A pleasant, embarrassing accident, but that's all. Or at least that's all it should have been.

A few years ago, while in Heidelberg, Germany, I had a free weekend to fill. Early Saturday morning I took a notebook and my German textbook and found a bench underneath a tree beside the Neckar River on which I proceeded to study German. I had been engrossed in my work for a while, and when I stopped to take a break from my work, I quickly noticed that the environment had changed. The place where I sat was in the vicinity of sunbathers, all of whom had apparently bought their swimwear on sale, because they were fifty percent off. It was a good time to find a different place to study.

Likewise, David should have discreetly walked away; but, instead, he chose to pursue Bathsheba and sent to inquire about her. What he heard should have stopped him instantly in his tracks. This beautiful young woman was the daughter of one of his best friends, Eliam, and wife of Uriah the Hittite, both of whom were members of David's trusted "band of men." They were both off at war, fighting for the cause of their friend, David. Her grandfather, Ahithophel, was David's number one advisor (2 Samuel 15:12).

Knowing full well who she was, David sent for her and took her to bed. As soon as they were done, she got up, took a bath, and went home. There was no love here; this was an expression of raw, physical lust.

Why David felt that he needed to do this escapes all logic. He was married at the time, with six wives as well as concubines (2 Samuel 5:13; 1 Chronicles 3:1–3). For some reason, David wanted Bathsheba more than all of these, and more than the friendship of his closest companions. What would possess a man to risk his family, his friendships, and his ministry for a few minutes of pleasure? Apparently, David was thinking that those few minutes of pleasure were worth the cost; or, more likely, David wasn't thinking at all.

I observe from this that *sin is deceptive,* and David believed a lie. Some of the lies that we hear today go like this: "No one will know."

"No one will care; we are two consenting adults." "It won't hurt anyone." "Just this once will be okay." "Nothing bad can happen to us." "Just wear a condom."

Sin distorts clear thinking. As Paul said,

You were dead in your trespasses and sins, in which you formerly walked according to the course of this world, according to the prince of the power of the air, of the spirit that is now working in the sons of disobedience. Among them we too formerly lived in the lusts of our flesh, indulging the desires of the flesh and of the mind, and were by nature children of wrath. (Ephesians 2:1–3)

In other words, there is a spirit or attitude that dominates the thought pattern of the world that leads people to indulge themselves with their fantasies rather than to think clearly and logically about what is happening.

The primary deception is that we all think of ourselves as the one exception to the rule, and that while no one else can, we will avoid facing the consequences of our actions. After my reconstructive knee surgery, my recovery was rapid, and I genuinely wanted to return to my normal regimen of strenuous physical activities. My doctor, however, who had seen hundreds of patients just like me, was blunt when he cautioned me not to be fooled into thinking that my knee was healed just because the pain was gone. His warning was right on target when he said, "Don't think that somehow you are the exception."

Within a few weeks of her encounter with David, Bathsheba started to notice that something was different. She woke up mornings feeling queasy and nauseous, and soon realized that her regular menstrual cycle was past due. She called David and told him the news. David was not overjoyed. Instead of openly admitting his sin right away, David proceeded to work out a plan to cover up for his treachery. He sent and brought Uriah, Bathsheba's husband, home from the battlefield for a little R and R, with the hope that her pregnancy could be attributed to Uriah.

Uriah did not think it was fair that he should be treated so favorably while everyone else was engaged in battle.

Uriah said to David, "The ark and Israel and Judah are staying in temporary shelters, and my lord Joab and the servants of my lord are camping in the open field. Shall I then go to my house to eat and to drink and to lie with my wife? By your life and the life of your soul, I will not do this thing." (2 Samuel 11:11)

Uriah refused to sleep with his wife.

On hearing Uriah's response, David must have been stabbed by guilt. Uriah's loyalty to David and his compatriots kept him from sleeping with his own wife, while David's loyalty to Uriah was nonexistent. While this should have made David repentant, it hardened David against Uriah, and David secretly scorned him.

David's stomach must have been in knots. His first attempt to hide his sin failed, so a second plan was quickly devised. He sent a letter to Joab, the commander of the army.

He had written in the letter, saying, "Place Uriah in the front line of the fiercest battle and withdraw from him, so that he may be struck down and die." (2 Samuel 11:15)

The purpose of David's plan was too obvious, because it was hastily drawn up, and was not the result of rational thinking. Trying to protect David, Joab changed the plan to avoid making Uriah's death look deliberate, with the result that additional Israelite soldiers died. How would David react to this loss of life and to the grieving of Israelite wives and children? Would David accuse Joab of poor military leadership?

[Joab] *charged the messenger, saying, "When you have finished telling all the events of the war to the king, and if it happens that the king's wrath rises and he says to you, 'Why did you go so near to the city to fight? Did you not know that they would shoot from the wall?' . . . , then you shall say, 'Your servant Uriah the Hittite is dead also.' "* (2 Samuel 11:19–21)

All that mattered to David was self-protection, covering up for his sin. He had lost all concern for his friends, his soldiers, and their families. He was a hardened, trapped man. We learn from this that *sin is enslaving.* With each event, David became more trapped and more desperate. One lie had to be covered by another, and his problems were escalating.

As soon as Bathsheba ended a time of mourning for Uriah, she and David were married. David breathed a sigh of relief, because the baby was now legitimized and no one would be the wiser—except anyone who could count to nine.

At this point, not many people knew what had happened, or at least not many people were talking openly about it. But God knew, and the sin, like all sin, could not remain hidden.

Do not be deceived, God is not mocked; for whatever a man sows, this he will also reap. (Galatians 6:7)

The justice of God is based on the very simple operating principle that people are allowed to experience the consequences of their choices, and are placed under the control of their lust's object (Ezekiel 23:9). What could be more fair? No one is condemned by God for something he or she did not willingly choose to do.

God revealed to the prophet Nathan the nature of this sin, and God sent Nathan to tell David the consequences. Usually we do not know in advance what the consequences of our own sin will be or how they will play out, but that does not change the fact that *the consequences of sin are inevitable.*

"Indeed you did it secretly, but I will do this thing before all Israel, and under the sun." (2 Samuel 12:12)

David paid a horrible price for his few minutes of pleasure. He became hardened against a dear friend, and bore the guilt of the death of innocent men, from which he never recovered. Nathan revealed four more things that would happen as a result of his compounded sin.

"The sword shall never depart from your house." (2 Samuel 12:10)

Indeed, his children were constantly at each other's throats. His oldest living son Amnon raped his daughter Tamar. Absalom, who was next in line for the throne behind Amnon, despised and eventually killed Amnon. David's children had no difficulty following his example of disrespect for women and friendship.

"I will raise up evil [i.e., rebellion] *against you from your own household."* (2 Samuel 12:11)

There was constant struggle for David's throne among his offspring. His son Absalom tried to take David's throne by force, and after Absalom's death, the heir-apparent, Adonijah, tried to take the throne, even though David had decided to appoint Solomon as his successor (1 Kings 1:5).

"I will even take your wives before your eyes, and give them to your companion, and he shall lie with your wives in broad daylight." (2 Samuel 12:11)

Before his rebellion was put down, Absalom had had sex with ten of David's concubines in a tent on the roof where everyone could see (2 Samuel 16:20–22). Why do you think he chose to place the tent on the roof? He did so at the advice of David's embittered, renegade advisor, Ahithophel, who never forgot the horror of what David had done to his lovely granddaughter Bathsheba and her husband Uriah.

"The child . . . that is born to you shall surely die." (2 Samuel 12:14)

But these four consequences of sin are simply what could be observed externally. We know from his poetry that David was living an emotional nightmare. He describes some of his agony in Psalm 51, where, reading between the lines, we see revealed the needs from which his requests sprang.

Wash me thoroughly from my iniquity, and cleanse me from my sin. (Psalm 51:2)

David felt horribly dirty and in need of thorough cleansing. He felt rotten to the core, because he was truly guilty, and no amount of self-justification could make him feel clean.

I know my transgressions, and my sin is ever before me. (Psalm 51:3)

He could not concentrate for any length of time on anything other than his sin. His thoughts hounded him day and night, and he was continually aware of the horrible facts of what he had done.

Against Thee, Thee only, have I sinned, and done what is evil in Thy sight, so that Thou art justified when Thou dost speak, and blameless when Thou dost judge. (Psalm 51:4)

His relationship with God was damaged and he knew that he stood guilty before the righteous Judge. But why did David say that this was a sin against God? After all, it was Uriah who was dead, and Bathsheba who was pregnant with an illegitimate child. Nathan explained:

"Thus says the LORD God of Israel, 'It is I who anointed you king over Israel and it is I who delivered you from the hand of Saul. I also gave you your master's house and your master's wives into your care, and I gave you the house of Israel and Judah; and if that had been too

little, I would have added to you many more things like these! Why have you despised the word of the LORD by doing evil in His sight?" (2 Samuel 12:7–9)

In other words, God had given David everything he needed and more, and if he had needed more, God would have willingly provided that, too. Isn't that enough? David, why did you not believe that God wanted only the best for you, and would provide for your needs?

These are good questions for all of us to ask ourselves. Most of us have so much more than we need and yet there are many times that we chase after things that we want and think we need, but which could not possibly give lasting peace and satisfaction.

*"By this deed you have given occasion to the enemies of the LORD to blaspheme." (*2 Samuel 12:14)

This sin, and indeed every sin, is ultimately against God. People suffer when we fail to live according to God's plan, but worse, God's name is blasphemed, and His suffering is deepest. *All* sin shows a preference for the momentary pleasures of the world over the eternal joy of fellowship with God. David, in these acts, showed that he felt that God was not trustworthy or capable of providing for his needs. Furthermore, failure to trust an all-loving, all-providing God gives credence to the blasphemous beliefs of God's detractors.

I was brought forth in iniquity, and in sin my mother conceived me. (Psalm 51:5)

It is a fact that illegitimate children often feel unloved, unwanted, and of little value. David felt that he, like the child that was growing in Bathsheba's womb, was illegitimate, and pretty worthless besides.

*Thou dost desire truth in the innermost being, and in the hidden part Thou wilt make me know wisdom. (*Psalm 51:6)

But at this moment, David had lost all good judgment, could not think straight, and did not trust his own decisions. David knew that it was on the inside, where other observers could not see, that his dishonesty rested.

Purify me with hyssop, and I shall be clean; wash me, and I shall be whiter than snow. (Psalm 51:7)

Because at this point, David was feeling filthy. Furthermore, he knew that there was nothing he could do for himself, no defense or justification that would make him clean again.

Make me to hear joy and gladness, let the bones which Thou hast broken rejoice. (Psalm 51:8)

The only music he could sing was the blues, and his whole body ached from his sorrow. I imagine that if he composed songs with his harp, it was in a minor key. He could not sleep well, his stomach was knotted, his muscles were tense, and he generally ached all over.

Create in me a clean heart, O God, and renew a steadfast spirit within me. (Psalm 51:10)

David's concentration was gone. At times when he would start some useful project, his memory would remind him of his past, and rob him of his ability to complete the task. He could not stick to anything, but was easily distracted. He knew that only God could restore him to emotional health and stability.

Do not cast me away from Thy presence, and do not take Thy Holy Spirit from me. (Psalm 51:11)

David no longer had a close relationship with friends. They did not trust him because, indeed, he was not trustworthy. How he could face Bathsheba or Joab without dropping his eyes, avoiding eye contact, I do not know. You see, guilt causes a person to live in constant fear of discovery, or rejection, or further consequences. David felt incredibly lonely and dejected, fearing that God Himself might abandon him. He had no one left but God, and if God should abandon him, what then?

Most people do not understand the horror of eternal separation from God. They joke about hell, thinking that while God will not be there, at least all of their friends will be. But the hell of hell is its loneliness and separation. Imagine living in an environment where you can do or have anything you want except contact with another human being. No voices in the street, no laughter, no smiles, no communication.

Moms with small children might think this would be Utopia for a day or two, or perhaps a week. I complain when my day at the office is filled with constant interruptions, thinking how nice it would be to have unbroken quiet. But after a month, or a year, or ten years, dragging on day after endless day and still no possibility for human contact, the loneliness would be overpowering. Just ask anyone who was a prisoner of war in Vietnam's "Hanoi Hilton" if separation from other people is pleasant.

Existence in total separation from God, the Designer, Creator, and Sustainer of all life, would be worse, infinitely worse. David understood that separation from God is hell.

Restore to me the joy of Thy salvation, and sustain me with a willing spirit. (Psalm 51:12)

David did not feel much joy at all, in fact, there was a lot of rebellion and unwillingness in his spirit. I have never met a happy rebel; rebels do not experience much joy.

I will teach transgressors Thy ways, and sinners will be converted to Thee. (Psalm 51:13)

As things were at the moment, there was nothing to say to anyone, and no one in their right mind would believe an adulterer and convicted murderer anyway. David's impact and sense of usefulness to God were completely gone. Yet he desired to once again be a person who could be trusted and who could help people find a meaningful relationship with God.

O LORD, open my lips, that my mouth may declare Thy praise. (Psalm 51:15)

But right now, David did not feel like saying much of anything, and did not have a whole lot to get excited about.

I see from this poem of David's that *sin is emotionally devastating.* Sin eats away at a person, and while he may try to hide it, ignore it, or forget it, sin eventually leads to emotional ruin.

This account illustrates at least five things that you can count on concerning sin:

1) Sin is opportunistic,

2) sin is deceptive,

3) sin is enslaving,

4) the consequences of sin are inevitable,

5) sin is emotionally devastating.

Søren Kierkegaard observed that it costs a man more to go to hell than to go to heaven, and the writer of the Proverbs (13:15) said that the way of the transgressor is hard. To depart from righteousness is to choose a life of crushing burdens, of failures and disappointment; a life caught in the toils of endless problems that are never resolved. Yet, while all of this is true, and its truth is seen in the broken lives of many people around us, if we ended here, we would be missing the most important point of the story, namely,

6) sin can be forgiven by God.

David said to Nathan, "I have sinned against the LORD." And Nathan said to David, "The LORD also has taken away your sin; you shall not die." (2 Samuel 12:13)

David's confession was short and to the point. David had heard the accusation of Nathan, knew what was going on inside his own head, and decided that the appropriate response was to confess his sin and seek forgiveness.

That is not the way everyone responds when confronted with the facts of their sin. Some people deny that they are sinners. The apostle John wrote about this kind of person.

> *If we say that we have fellowship with Him and yet walk in darkness, we lie and do not practice the truth.* (1 John 1:6)
>
> *If we say that we have no sin, we are deceiving ourselves and the truth is not in us.* (1 John 1:8)
>
> *If we say that we have not sinned, we make Him a liar, and His word is not in us.* (1 John 1:10)

In other words, if we say that there is nothing wrong with ourselves, we are calling God a liar, making us *heretics*, we are fooling ourselves, not facing reality, making us *psychotics*, and we are trying (unsuccessfully) to fool other people, making us *hypocrites*.

Of course, we may recognize our sin, but decide to keep it hidden and try to live with it. After all, what's the big deal about not being perfect?

Scripture makes it clear that trying to cover up our sin is also futile. To act as if nothing is wrong is draining and saps us of all our energy.

> *He who conceals his transgressions will not prosper.* (Proverbs 28:13)
>
> *When I kept silent about my sin, my body wasted away through my groaning all day long. For day and night Thy hand was heavy upon me; my vitality was drained away as with the fever-heat of summer.* (Psalm 32:3–4)

What is to be done about my sin? It is illogical to deny that it exists. It is futile to try to hide it. The only reasonable thing to do is exactly what David did, to confess it and forsake it. God will not turn his back on a person who is genuinely sorry for his sin.

He who confesses and forsakes them will find compassion. (Proverbs 28:13b)

The sacrifices of God are a broken spirit; a broken and a contrite heart, O God, Thou wilt not despise. (Psalm 51:17)

I acknowledged my sin to Thee, and my iniquity I did not hide; I said, "I will confess my transgressions to the LORD"; and Thou didst forgive the guilt of my sin. (Psalm 32:5)

The last part of this verse makes an important point. It says that God will forgive the *guilt* of our sin, but it does not say that God will reverse the *consequences* of our sin. In fact, as it was with David, it is often the case that people must live with the consequences of their sin for years.

Indescribable are the feelings of relief and exuberant joy that come when a person understands that his guilt has been completely forgiven, that he is released from the crush of guilt inflicted torture.

How blessed is he whose transgression is forgiven, whose sin is covered! How blessed is the man to whom the LORD does not impute iniquity, and in whose spirit there is no deceit! (Psalm 32:1–2)

Sin exacts a horrible price. Sin never misses an opportunity to take advantage of you, to deceive you, to enslave you, and to destroy you. The physical and emotional consequences of sin are destructive and inevitable. But the grace of God is greater by far than all of our sin, and forgiveness is available to anyone who is willing to readily confess his sin and to accept God's plan for forgiveness. The consequences of sin are hideous, but God's forgiveness is total; you can count on it!

Study Guide for Chapter 6

1. For content:
• Read 2 Samuel 11–12.

• What are five things that you can count on concerning sin?

• Make a list of the emotional and psychological struggles David had as a result of his guilt (review Psalm 51).

• What are the advantages of staying clean before God (review Proverbs 28:13b; Psalm 51:17; and Psalm 32:1–2, 5).

2. For further study:
• According to Hosea 4:1–3 what suffers when sin is allowed to continue unchecked?

• The cost of discipleship is far less than the price of sin. How does Jesus express this idea in Matthew 11:28–30? In the long run, which is easier: to confess and forsake, or to ignore and conceal our sin?

• How does Paul describe the penalty for disobedience of God in 2 Thessalonians 1:9? Why is this a horrible price to pay?

3. For application:
• To which of the emotions expressed in Psalm 51 do you relate best?

• Give a personal illustration (as a metaphor) of how dirtiness affects personal relationships. For example, describe an embarrassing encounter you've had just after a garlic-laden meal or after strenuous exercise where your personal hygiene affected your relationships with people.

• What reasons can you find to explain why we sometimes choose to stay in sin when we know the benefits of being clean? What makes confession of sin difficult?

4. For action:
• For one week, clip articles from your local newspaper that mention the consequences of sin. (Don't expect the articles to actually identify sin as such! You will need to make that identification for yourself.) Do the articles deal with the problem by ignoring it, finding a scapegoat, or acknowledging that it is the consequence of previous behavior?

• Describe how sin was dealt with in the last movie that you saw. Identify sins that went unchecked and were glamorized. Were the consequences of sin shown or ignored?

* Read *The Screwtape Letters* by C. S. Lewis.

5. For personal commitment:
3-by-5: Memorize Psalm 51:15–17.

7.

What Went Wrong?

Joshua 9, 23

"Choose for yourselves today whom you will serve; . . . but as for me and my house, we will serve the LORD."—Joshua 24:15

It is unlikely that I will ever become wealthy overnight. I do not play the lottery, and I have no rich uncles or aunts. I have had plenty of offers of free gifts, which on closer inspection were not really gifts, nor were they truly free. But imagine with me for a minute some of the thoughts that might run through your mind if you were to receive an unexpected call from a lawyer asking you to appear at the reading of the will of a distant relative.

"I wonder what he left for me." "I'll bet he gave most of it to my dreadful excuse for a cousin." "There is probably a catch. After all, there is no such thing as a free lunch." "I wonder if I should even go to the reading of the will. I'd hate to miss work."

Sure!

I can think of two ways that you could be an heir to a large estate and yet not enjoy the full benefits of the inheritance. It might be that you had to show up at the reading of the will to claim the inheritance, or else the estate would pass to someone else. And, on that particular day, you were too busy, or afraid of traveling on a plane to a strange city, and decided not to go.

Or it could be that there were some conditions to the inheritance, and if they were not adhered to, the inheritance would revert to a trust fund to be dispersed to your children on their coming of age. The conditions were simple enough, but you did not thoroughly understand them or chose to ignore them, and so fell into violation of its terms, thereby losing the benefits of inheritance.

These summarize fairly accurately the situation for many Christians. As children of God we are joint-heirs with Christ of all the benefits that go with having God as our Father. Yet many Christians do not appreciate all that this means, or know how to live in full enjoyment of their inheritance. It is as if they missed out on the reading of the will, or have rescinded some of the inheritance because they did not understand all of its conditions.

The benefits of being an heir of God are truly exciting. For example, in Joshua 1:1–5, God's promise of inheritance to the nation of Israel is summarized.

Moses My servant is dead; now therefore arise, cross this Jordan, you and all this people, to the land which I am giving to them, to the sons of Israel. Every place on which the sole of your foot treads, I have given it to you, just as I spoke to Moses. From the wilderness and this Lebanon, even as far as the great river, the river Euphrates, all the land of the Hittites, and as far as the Great Sea toward the setting of the sun, will be your territory. No man will be able to stand before you all the days of your life. Just as I have been with Moses, I will be with you; I will never fail you or forsake you. (Joshua 1:2–5)

In these verses God promises to give the Israelites their own land, and to get this land all they would have to do is show up. No one would be able to stand up to them, and God would continually be with them and would not forsake them. The land was a free gift, God had established them as the owners of it, and if they did not have possession of it, there was one very simple explanation: They had failed to show up.

Perhaps there were good reasons for not showing up, like stark terror. The problem for the Israelites, of course, was that there were giants living in the land, and these giants were well-entrenched. The societies that were already there were well-established, with fierce warriors who seemed to have a significant upper hand. There was clearly good reason to be afraid, and three times God encouraged Joshua not to be afraid, but to be strong and courageous. God also reminded Joshua of three things to help him maintain his attitude of strength and courage.

> *"Be strong and courageous, for you shall give this people possession of the land which I swore to their fathers to give them. Only be strong and very courageous; be careful to do according to all the law which Moses My servant commanded you; do not turn from it to the right or to the left, so that you may have success wherever you go. This book of the law shall not depart from your mouth, but you shall meditate on it day and night, so that you may be careful to do according to all that is written in it; for then you will make your way prosperous, and then you will have success. Have I not commanded you? Be strong and courageous! Do not tremble or be dismayed, for the LORD your God is with you wherever you go."* (Joshua 1:6–9)

First of all, Joshua, *God has promised to give you this land.* God does not go back on His promises. Furthermore, do not forget that *God is with you wherever you go*; He will not forsake you. However, you must be careful to know and think about and *obey God's laws.* Keep them uppermost in your mind and highest on your list of priorities. They were designed to make you prosperous and successful so that you could enjoy the full benefits of the promise.

Life is really no different for us than it was for Joshua. To the Christian, God has promised significant benefits as our inheritance, and they are offered freely as a gift. Attributes like love, joy, peace, patience, kindness, goodness, faithfulness, gentleness, and self-control. But there are giants in the land; obstacles that keep us from taking full advantage of what God has given us; habits, frustrations, and pitfalls that make us jealous, angry, or depressed. To take possession of our inheritance we need to face the giant head-on, be strong and courageous, and not discouraged or disheartened. Facing the giant of a bad habit, a bitter attitude, or discontented spirit requires strength and fortitude. But God promised victory over these things, and He has promised to always be with us, so why should we back away? If we get to know His Word and His way and live in obedience to Him by letting them thoroughly permeate our life, we cannot fail, not because of our own determination, but because it is the Spirit of the living God who indwells and empowers us and will overcome our most dreaded enemies.

So how did it turn out for Joshua?

The LORD gave Israel all the land which He had sworn to give to their fathers, and they possessed it and lived in it. And the LORD gave them rest on every side, according to all that He had sworn to their fathers, and no one of all their enemies stood before them; the LORD gave all their enemies into their hand. Not one of the good promises which the LORD had made to the house of Israel failed; all came to pass. (Joshua 21:43–45)

All of God's promises came to pass; all of their enemies were subdued and the land came into their possession. During the overthrow of thirty-one kings, the only loss of life to the Israelites occurred at Ai, where Achan and his family failed to follow orders. Sounds pretty good, doesn't it? You might imagine that no one would change a thing. If it works, don't fix it!

Unfortunately, things did not stay so good, but rapidly deteriorated after the end of Joshua's life. The warning signs of deterioration were already evident while Joshua was still alive. We would do well to figure out where the whole thing started to fall apart. Why did the heirs of God's promise not experience the full benefit of their inheritance?

In Joshua 23, Joshua gave his final address to the nation of Israel. Before his death, he reminded them of their memories of the amazing faithfulness of God in fighting for them, and challenged them to continue to follow God. In a forceful and dynamic way, he encouraged them to be firm in their adherence to God's Word, not to wander from it in any direction. To keep this steadfast dedication to God, they were not to associate with the nations around them, or become involved with any of the gods of the land, or adopt any of their religious practices, or let their religious vocabulary be influenced by other groups, or in any way become involved in adoration and worship of other gods. Here is how he put it:

> *Be very firm, then, to keep and do all that is written in the book of the law of Moses, so that you may not turn aside from it to the right hand or to the left, in order that you may not associate with these nations, these which remain among you, . . .*
>
> *If you ever go back and cling to the rest of these nations, these which remain among you, and intermarry with them, so that you associate with them and they with you, know with certainty that the LORD your God will not continue to drive these nations out from before you; but they shall be a snare and a trap to you, and a whip on your sides and thorns in your eyes, until you perish from off this good land which the LORD your God has given you.* (Joshua 23:6–7,12–13)

The principle for us is clear. If you want to have continued victory over the enemy and continued enjoyment of what God has given you, do not let the enemy's values influence yours. Keep yourself untainted from the practices and thought patterns of other religions and philosophies. As soon as you begin to lose your distinctives, and begin to look and act and think like the culture around you, three things will happen. *God will no longer fight your battles for you.* You will find that *the surrounding culture becomes a constant irritation to you.* You will not be able to see things clearly or walk freely, but *you will be constantly driven by the pressures of society.* As a result, you will no longer be in control, but will actually lose what you had gained as you are driven out of the land and are ultimately destroyed by the enemy. Even though you own the land, you will not possess or enjoy it.

It is so easy to lose our distinctives and become exactly like everyone else. We want houses and cars and income and vacation condos like everyone else, and before long we sense that we are struggling on our own to keep all of these things, barely able to stay afloat, and we feel that God is not fighting for us, because our goals are not God's goals. We become worried about rebellious teenagers, overanxious for a job promotion, driven by debt. (I owe, I owe, so off to work I go!) We are so driven by pressures at work that we have no time for our family or friends. Just as Joshua predicted, the surrounding culture has become a source of irritation and we are being constantly driven by the pressures of society.

For Israel, the process was gradual and subtle, but deadly. Coming from Egypt, the Israelites were familiar with an agricultural system that was based on the flooding of the Nile. But when they came to Canaan, they had to learn a whole new system of agriculture, and who better to learn it from than the people who were already successfully living there? If it works for them it must be fine for us. So the Canaanites instructed the Israelites on how to do dry farming, when to plant crops, when to plow fields to take best advantage of the seasonal rains. Of course, in the Canaanite view, their agricultural success was attributed to their pagan fertility rites, and so they taught these to the Israelites as well. Before long the Israelites had adopted the idol worship and perverted sexual practices of the Canaanites.

Moses foresaw the difficulty that would come to the Israelites if they allowed the values of the local culture to influence theirs. In Deuteronomy 7:1–5 he gave the same clear warning that was echoed later by Joshua, namely that they should not allow the people living in the land to turn them to following other gods.

When the LORD your God shall deliver them before you, and you shall defeat them, then you shall utterly destroy them. You shall make no covenant with them and show no favor to them. (Deuteronomy 7:2)

But wait a minute! It does not require careful reading to see that there is a major difference between what Moses said and what Joshua said. Joshua said that the Israelites should not associate with the people who remain in the land, but Moses did not mention any people who are left in the land. Moses clearly instructed them to utterly destroy the inhabitants of Canaan, to make no covenants with them and to completely eliminate all evidence of their religious practices. In Moses' view, none of the previous inhabitants were to be left after the Israelites moved in.

Why is there such a difference between Moses' command and Joshua's? Is it that Moses was a hardened old man, but Joshua was a more moderate, reasonable and realistic political leader? No. In fact, Joshua was in a compromised situation that was already having its effect on his ability to lead effectively.

Moses' command to completely destroy the inhabitants of the land was not cruel or unjust. The Canaanite culture was arguably the most degraded culture that has ever existed. It was openly committed to cruelty (child sacrifice was common) and perverted sexual practices (recall that the word *sodomy* comes from the name of the city of Sodom, which had earlier been destroyed), so that venereal disease was rampant. Certainly, many children were born suffering from the effects, such as blindness, of sexually transmitted diseases. The Baals were fertility gods, and Ashtoreth was a female sex symbol. Phallic symbols as religious objects of worship were prevalent throughout the culture. Male and female cult prostitutes populated their temples.

Life had gone on like this for well over four hundred years, and by the time the Israelites approached its borders, the society was in collapse as a natural consequence of its own evil. In Genesis 15:16, God told Abraham that his descendants would be slaves in a foreign land for four hundred years before they could return to Canaan, because "the iniquity of the Amorite is not yet complete." In other words, God knew that the Canaanite culture was evil and collapsing, but before He would destroy it, their iniquity had to be complete, that is, so totally degraded that there could be no question that its destruction was deserved and required.

When he entered the land, Joshua knew quite well the command of Moses. He had read all of the law of Moses to the people right after the destruction of Ai.

He read all the words of the law, the blessing and the curse, according to all that is written in the book of the law. There was not a word of all that Moses had commanded which Joshua did not read before all the assembly of Israel with the women and the little ones and the strangers who were living among them. (Joshua 8:34–35)

Unfortunately, this did not prevent the leaders of Israel from making a serious mistake soon thereafter.

By the time Jericho and Ai had been captured and destroyed, the progress of the Israelites was well known to the remaining inhabitants of Canaan, and they began to devise ways to survive this advance. Six of the threatened nations allied themselves into one massive army to fight against Israel. The inhabitants of Gibeon came up with another plan (Joshua 9). They dressed a number of their men in rags, gave them torn and worn out bags, wineskins, and sandals, gave them stale bread, and sent them to see Joshua. I imagine they chose only skinny men. As they stumbled into the Israelite camp at Gilgal, they gave the impression that they had come a long distance, and they offered the terms of a treaty to become servants of Israel without a fight.

So Joshua made a covenant with them, allowing them to live. Of course, within a few days Joshua discovered that these people were neighbors (they lived less than ten miles from Ai), and the Israelites' dilemma became obvious. They could not destroy these men because they had given their word, and they could not obey God's command because they had made a conflicting covenant with the Gibeonites.

There are three things to notice about this agreement. First, it was based on the lie that these people had come from a distant place and were destitute. The scheme was craftily conceived and carried out, and it depended on the believability of a lie. Second, the decision seemed logical enough. After all, wouldn't it be better to have able-bodied slaves than corpses? Having slaves could make their life so much better. Furthermore, it is more convenient to sign a peace pact than to fight a war. Finally, the decision was made without consulting God. Even though they had just read the law of Moses, they did not check to see what God had to say about this agreement. The bottom line was that this agreement was in direct disobedience to a command of God: They were to make no covenants.

Compromises today are similar. After all, the things that our society offers us are so neatly packaged and paraded in front of us. We are constantly being told that we can be happier, slimmer, sexier, or healthier if we simply buy some new and wonderful product. But it is a craftily conceived lie! Sorry, but it is not true that you will have more sex appeal if you switch to using the right toothpaste or drinking the right beer. Your life will not necessarily be easier if you have the latest and greatest time-saving device. After being bombarded with these messages for a while, it seems so logical, or perhaps we no longer care whether it is logical or not. We buy into the lie. Just like the Israelites, we fail to carefully examine if what is said is true or if this is something God has warned against. We fail to think carefully about the relevance of God's Word to our decisions even though we hear it preached or taught in church week after week. Little by little our distinctives are lost.

The real problem with compromise, as Joshua discovered, is that it is an attempt to serve two masters. Joshua could not honor the agreement he had made with the Gibeonites and be obedient to God at the same time. The fact is that if we are not totally obedient to God, we are therefore not serving Him, so we must be serving something else.

It may not appear at the moment to be servitude, but the progression is clear. In the lives of the Israelites (read Judges 1:22–36), the slaves gradually became the masters, and for us, an apparent asset gradually becomes a liability.

Even though Joshua's disobedience placed him in a difficult position, he understood clearly the issues that were involved. He knew that the decisions we make are consequences of the God we serve. He also knew that we have to make a choice: either serve the gods of the age or the God of the Ages.

The issue today is no less clear. We have to decide whom we will serve, and then act in consistency with that decision. If we want God to fight our battles, and if we want to experience all the benefits of life in God's kingdom, we must obey and serve only God. But, as with the Israelites, the number one reason we do not experience the victorious Christian life as God designed it is because we are unwilling to rid ourselves of the demands of other gods, gods like my rights, my career, money, possessions, or leisure activity.

Here's the point. When we make compromises to the standards of the world around us, life does not get easier, it gets harder. We become less satisfied with our job, with our income, with our family, and with our friends because we have allowed our culture's standards to infiltrate ours. When we accept their definition of prosperity and success, we become dissatisfied with the way to which our needs are being attended. When we accept our culture's definition of acceptance we find ourselves seeking popularity and fame rather than the depth of relationship offered in the family of God. When we accept the world's definition of sexual satisfaction we find ourselves trapped in a world of fantasy and delusion that in no way compares to the fulfillment offered in a God-designed marriage relationship. Mixing our values with the values of the world makes us miserable and defeated, not joyful and content. When that happens, just as Joshua said,

1) God no longer goes to battle for us,
2) society becomes a constant irritant,
3) we cannot escape its relentless pressure.

No one I know loses sleep worrying about Canaanites or Per-izzites or Jebusites. People lose sleep because of bills that have not been paid, promotions that were deserved but not received, or sex that was denied. Our sleeplessness and tension headaches come because we have allowed the values of the culture around us to infiltrate and distort godly values. We have adopted their values with regard to money management, sexuality, and career development, and God no longer fights these battles for us. The -ites of this age have become thorns in our eyes and whips in our sides, so that we cry ourselves into restless sleep.

Joshua's answer is as valid for us today as it was for the Israelites. If we want to have the full benefit of being a child of God, and full access to His resources in our lives, we must make a choice. As Joshua said,

> *"Choose for yourselves today whom you will serve; . . . but as for me and my house, we will serve the LORD."* (Joshua 24:15)

Study Guide for Chapter 7

1. For content:
• Read Joshua 9.

• What were the promises of God to Joshua and the Israelites?

• What were the conditions enabling them to enjoy the full benefit of the promises?

• What were some of the factors leading to Joshua's decision to make a covenant with the Gibeonites?

2. For further study:
• What are the riches that we have inherited through Christ Jesus, as described by the apostle Paul in Ephesians 1:7–8, 18–19; 2:4–7?

• What are the practical implications of Romans 13:8? What kind of indebtedness does Paul encourage?

* Read Genesis 15–16. What kept Abraham and Sarah from enjoying the full benefit of God's promise to them? In what way did they take on a slave who eventually became their master?

3. For application:
• In what ways is our society encouraging you to take on more slaves?

• How is it that slaves can become masters? Give an example of this from your own life (for instance, credit cards, home equity loans, time-saving devices, free time, or diet/exercise programs).

• What are some reasons that we compromise to the world's standards on Monday morning even when we have heard God's Word preached on Sunday?

• How do peer pressure and time pressures help or hinder you in making God-directed decisions?

• What would it take for you to get completely out of debt? How would you have to scale down your current lifestyle to live debt-free? What advantages do you see to being debt-free? What problems?

4. For action:
• Watch a late-night television newscast and record on paper all advertised products and the premise for its appeal according to advertisers. How many of the advertisements are completely honest and factual, and how many are misrepresenting the truth or promoting a falsehood?

• Keep a list of all the offers you receive in one week to take on more slaves.

5. For personal commitment:
3-by-5: Memorize Joshua 24:15.

8.

The High Cost of Disobedience

1 Samuel 13, 15

Whatever you may do, don't put the blame on you; blame it on the rain.—Milli Vanilli

My ears always perk up when my son runs into my study and proclaims, "It's not my fault, Dad. I didn't do it." With such an introduction, I am predisposed to believe that he did do something, and that it was his fault. Children are full of ready excuses for every occasion. "I had a phone call," "But my sister hasn't done her homework yet, either," and "Mom told me to go to the store instead," have all been heard in our home at one time or another. The three words that every mom most longs to hear are "My room's clean," but usually all they hear are excuses for why it is not. As a friend once said, "It isn't whether you win or lose that matters, it's how you place the blame."

King Saul was a man who had plenty of excuses for his disobedience to God, but it cost him dearly. On a number of occasions, he did things that were in direct disobedience to a command of God.

The first of these occasions is recorded in 1 Samuel 13. Relationships between the Philistines and Israel were difficult during the time of Saul. Whenever they could, the Israelites tried to inflict damage upon the Philistines, who were encroaching upon Israelite territory. We read in 1 Samuel 13:3 that, shortly after Saul's inauguration as king of Israel, his son Jonathan made a raid on a garrison of Philistine soldiers at Geba, inflicting serious damage. This attack incited the wrath of the Philistines, who then gathered in large numbers in reaction to the attack.

Even though Saul was a large man and looked like he would be a good soldier, he was still new at the job and his military leadership was unproven. The people were not confident in his leadership, saw that they were in serious trouble, and were terrified. They hid themselves wherever they could, in caves, thickets, cliffs, cellars, or in pits. Some even crossed eastward over the Jordan River to escape the Philistine threat. The group of people whom Saul had recruited to stay with him were trembling with fear. Saul needed to do something to bolster the confidence of the people; but there was a further problem. The prophet Samuel had told him to do nothing until Samuel arrived, and Samuel had promised to arrive within seven days. Samuel had made a similar request of Saul previously, so Saul was familiar with this kind of request.

Saul knew that Samuel intended to offer sacrifices in preparation for their impending battle with the Philistines, as this was the way the Israelites were always supposed to begin their preparations for war (Deuteronomy 20). But the seven days seemed to last forever, Samuel was running late, and the people were deserting in droves. Out of desperation, Saul offered the burnt offering himself.

Saul had seen the burnt offering sacrificed before, so he knew how to carry out the ritual, but Saul was not qualified to make the offering. The priest was the only one who could offer the sacrifice, and Saul was the king, not the priest.

Wouldn't you know it, as soon as Saul had finished offering the sacrifice, Samuel showed up. Perhaps Samuel was a few minutes late, or Saul was a few minutes early. Either way, Saul had done something that he knew he should not have done. He ran out to greet Samuel to begin damage control.

Perhaps there was still smoke in the air when Samuel and Saul met. Immediately upon meeting, Samuel asked Saul a simple question.

"What have you done?" (1 Samuel 13:11)

Saul knew that he had done something wrong, as shown by his defensive answer.

And Saul said, "Because I saw that the people were scattering from me, and that you did not come within the appointed days, and that the Philistines were assembling at Michmash, therefore I said, 'Now the Philistines will come down against me at Gilgal, and I have not asked the favor of the LORD.' So I forced myself and offered the burnt offering." (1 Samuel 13:11–12)

What a nice list of excuses! The people were leaving because they were afraid, Samuel was late, the Philistines were amassing for an attack, and Saul did not want to do anything that was not blessed by God. Saul did not want it to happen this way, but his hand had been forced. The people were to blame, Samuel was to blame, the Philistines were to blame, God was to blame, but Saul was innocent, at least in his own eyes.

But wait a minute, Saul. With all of your impeccable logic and thorough scapegoating, you forgot one thing. Did you do what God asked you to do, yes or no?

Samuel said to Saul, "You have acted foolishly; you have not kept the commandment of the LORD your God, which He commanded you, for now the LORD would have established your kingdom over Israel forever. But now your kingdom shall not endure." (1 Samuel 13:13–14a)

The summary statement is succinct, but clear. It may have seemed logical at the time, but if it is not in obedience to God, it is foolish. All the logic in the world does not obviate the need for obedience to God.

Furthermore, because of disobedience to God, your kingdom will not be established. That is, as soon as your life is over, so is your impact. There will be no permanence to your accomplishments. As far as God is concerned, you and your accomplishments will be here today, gone tomorrow.

We learn from this that *a life that is not lived in obedience to God does not count for much,* and in God's eyes does not have a lasting impact.

Some time later, Samuel approached Saul again with another set of instructions.

Samuel said to Saul, "The LORD sent me to anoint you as king over His people, over Israel; now therefore, listen to the words of the LORD. Thus says the LORD of hosts, 'I will punish Amalek for what he did to Israel, how he set himself against him on the way while he was coming up from Egypt. Now go and strike Amalek and utterly destroy all that he has, and do not spare him; but put to death both man and woman, child and infant, ox and sheep, camel and donkey.' " (1 Samuel 15:1–3)

The Amalekites were a Bedouin-like tribe of nomads living in the southeastern desert, whose treachery is well documented. Amalek was the grandson of Esau and one of his wives Adah, a Hittite. Aside from the fact that descendants of Esau never seemed to get along well with descendants of Jacob (a.k.a. Israel), the real difficulty between the Amalekites and the Israelites began sometime during the first two months after the Exodus from Egypt. The Amalekites struck the refugee Israelites from behind, attacking primarily stragglers, those who were tired or old and incapable of self-defense. Although Joshua led a successful counterattack, God made a promise to Joshua at the time that the memory of Amalek would eventually be totally wiped out.

Later the Amalekites aligned themselves with the Moabites, and during the time of Gideon, they cooperated with the Midianites in carrying out raids on Israelite communities. Throughout their history, they were opportunistic pests, exploiting the weaknesses of their opponents whenever possible. The command to Saul to utterly destroy the Amalekites was justified by their history of treachery (Romans 3:5).

So Saul struck out against the Amalekites, and he destroyed everything. Well, almost everything.

But Saul and the people captured Agag [the king of the Amalekites] *and the best of the sheep, the oxen, the fatlings, the lambs, and all that was good, and were not willing to destroy them utterly; but everything despised and worthless, that they utterly destroyed.* (1 Samuel 15:9)

Saul had his own criteria for what should be destroyed, and in his estimation, there were a number of things that should be spared. I guess he figured that he knew better than God what was the appropriate fate for the people and the animals.

God informed Samuel of Saul's action, so Samuel came to Saul with a message from God. Saul opened the conversation.

"Blessed are you of the LORD! I have carried out the command of the LORD." (1 Samuel 15:13)

That was a lie, and Samuel knew it, not only because God had revealed it to him, but because of the wafting from just over the hill of an array of animal sounds.

Samuel said, "What then is this bleating of the sheep in my ears, and the lowing of the oxen which I hear?" (1 Samuel 15:14)

Saul was caught with the goods. But that was no problem; he had a few excuses ready.

Saul said, "They have brought them from the Amalekites, for the people spared the best of the sheep and oxen, to sacrifice to the LORD your God; but the rest we have utterly destroyed." (1 Samuel 15:15)

First of all, it was the people's fault; they were the ones who rounded up the animals and brought them here. Furthermore, they kept only the best animals so that they could be sacrificed to God. In other words, it was someone else's doing, and it was for a good cause.

Saul seemed not to understand the word *sacrifice*. It is no sacrifice to give up that which is not mine, or to give to God something that costs me nothing (2 Samuel 24:24). When the police take a stolen stereo away from a thief to return it to its rightful owner, the thief cannot claim that he made a tremendous sacrifice for the benefit of the owner (Malachi 1:13). Furthermore, there is no value in religious activity or ritual if it is in a context of disobedience to God.

I hate, I reject your festivals, nor do I delight in your solemn assemblies. Even though you offer up to Me burnt offerings and your grain offerings, I will not accept them; I will not even look at the peace offerings of your fatlings. Take away from Me the noise of your songs; I will not even listen to the sound of your harps. But let justice roll down like waters and righteousness like an ever-flowing stream. (Amos 5:21–24)

But I think that Saul no longer cared about pleasing God, because in talking to Samuel he referred to God as the Lord *your* God, instead of the Lord *my* God. Furthermore, it is evident from the passage that Saul had no intention of sacrificing those animals, at least until Samuel came along. Saul wanted the animals for himself. He probably also kept King Agag alive for his own political purposes. Notice (1 Samuel 15:12) that Saul built a monument to himself immediately after the victory. He was evidently quite pleased with himself.

But Saul failed to understand an important principle about desiring things that God had determined should be destroyed.

As for you, only keep yourselves from the things under the ban, lest you covet them and take some of the things under the ban, so you would make the camp of Israel accursed and bring trouble on it. (Joshua 6:18)

You see, there are some things that other people have that are not worth having, even though they sometimes may appear to be very desirable. No matter how well-written the articles are, it is not enough to justify buying a copy of *Playboy*. There are some things that we simply should not have in our homes, because if we do let them in, they bring only curses and trouble.

Samuel relayed to Saul what he had heard from God the previous night.

Samuel said, "Is it not true, though you were little in your own eyes, you were made the head of the tribes of Israel? And the LORD *anointed you king over Israel, and the* LORD *sent you on a mission, and said, 'Go and utterly destroy the sinners, the Amalekites, and fight against them until they are exterminated.' Why then did you not obey the voice of the* LORD, *but rushed upon the spoil and did what was evil in the sight of the* LORD?" (1 Samuel 15:17–19)

Saul insists upon his innocence.

Saul said to Samuel, "I did obey the voice of the LORD, *and went on the mission on which the* LORD *sent me, and have brought back Agag the king of Amalek, and have utterly destroyed the Amalekites. But the people took some of the spoil, sheep and oxen, the choicest of the things devoted to destruction, to sacrifice to the* LORD *your God at Gilgal." (1 Samuel 15:20–21)

Saul's excuse was the same. It was their fault, not his. Samuel had heard enough.

Samuel said, "Has the LORD as much delight in burnt offerings and sacrifices as in obeying the voice of the LORD? Behold, to obey is better than sacrifice, and to heed than the fat of rams. For rebellion is as the sin of divination, and insubordination is as iniquity and idolatry. Because you have rejected the word of the LORD, He has rejected you from being king." (1 Samuel 15:22–23)

There may be married couples who insist that their fights are worthwhile because making up is so much fun, but that is not the way God operates. Restoring a relationship is hard work and very costly. Maintaining the relationship is to be much preferred over trying to heal the wounds caused during the heat of an argument.

Why does Samuel equate rebellion and insubordination (i.e., disobedience) with divination and idolatry? Divination is nothing more than appealing to another god for guidance, and idolatry (which is equated with harlotry throughout the Old Testament) is the same as seeking out another god for our satisfaction and pleasures. When we disobey God, we are making the statement that God is not able to guide us or to adequately fill our needs or to give us pleasure.

Saul's disobedience was, in fact, obedience to another god, whom he believed (or so his actions implied) could better guide him, provide for him, and give him fulfillment. Saul's god was people.

Saul said to Samuel, "I have sinned; I have indeed transgressed the command of the LORD and your words, because I feared the people and listened to their voice. (1 Samuel 15:24)

It is the consequence of Saul's disobedience that needs emphasis here. Because Saul would not obey God, he was disqualified from being king. Does that seem backward to you, that one of the qualifications of living like a king is being obedient? Perhaps you thought that living like a king meant being above all the rules by being the one who made the rules. No, in God's kingdom, to live like a king, one must learn obedience to the King of kings.

Living in disobedience to God disqualifies us from living like kings. That is, we miss out on the full benefit of being a child of the King, and of living the way God intended us to live. In other words, *people who are not obedient to God cannot be truly fulfilled,* because they cannot enjoy all of their inheritance as a child of God.

Unfortunately, the story does not end here. As is so often true, the full effect of a person's disobedience is not apparent until many years later. In 1 Samuel 31, we learn about the battle against the Philistines in which Saul lost his life. The battle was fought in the region of Mt. Gilboa, in northern Israel, near the places where God had given spectacular victories to Deborah and Barak over Sisera at Kishon, and to Gideon against the Midianites at Jezreel. But God was not fighting this battle for Saul, and the result was only despair and agony for Israel.

The Philistines were fighting against Israel, and the men of Israel fled from before the Philistines and fell slain on Mount Gilboa. And the Philistines overtook Saul and his sons; and the Philistines killed Jonathan and Abinadab and Malchi-shua the sons of Saul. And the battle went heavily against Saul, and the archers hit him; and he was badly wounded by the archers. Then Saul said to his armor bearer, "Draw your sword and pierce me through with it, lest these uncircumcised come and pierce me through and make sport of me." But his armor bearer would not, for he was greatly afraid. So Saul took his sword and fell on it. And when his armor bearer saw that Saul was dead, he also fell on his sword and died with him. Thus Saul died with his three sons, his armor bearer, and all his men on that day together. (1 Samuel 31:1–6)

Saul died a despondent man, having to commit suicide to prevent being tortured to death by the Philistines, his number one enemy. At the same time, three of his sons were killed. His personal bodyguard was so desperately afraid of what might happen to him as a prisoner of war that he also committed suicide. As it does so often, the consequences of one man's disobedience ultimately affected innocent family and friends.

Many Israelites were disgraced and discouraged when Saul fell. They fled for their lives, and territory that had previously been captured was lost back to the Philistines.

When the men of Israel who were on the other side of the valley, with those who were beyond the Jordan, saw that the men of Israel had fled and that Saul and his sons were dead, they abandoned the cities and fled; then the Philistines came and lived in them. (1 Samuel 31:7)

The Philistines made the most of their victory.

It came about on the next day when the Philistines came to strip the slain, that they found Saul and his three sons fallen on Mount Gilboa. And they cut off his head, and stripped off his weapons, and sent them throughout the land of the Philistines, to carry the good news to the house of their idols and to the people. And they put his weapons in the temple of Ashtoreth, and they fastened his body to the wall of Bethshan. (1 Samuel 31:8–10)

Every religion has a message that it attempts to proclaim. Some non-Christian religions are so bold as to call their message the "gospel," which means the "good news" or "good story." The Philistines viewed the good news of their victory over Saul as a religious victory, and their gods received honor and praise as a result. On the day that Saul fell, a false religion had a heyday. It works that way today as well, when a major religious leader falls, because of sexual or ethical misdeeds, that the media have a field day and the false gods of our society are triumphant. The apparent failure of Christianity is always good press.

Saul's tragic death also led to heartache and personal sacrifice for a number of dedicated Israelites.

When the inhabitants of Jabesh-gilead heard what the Philistines had done to Saul, all the valiant men rose and walked all night, and took the body of Saul and the bodies of his sons from the wall of Beth-

shan, and they came to Jabesh, and burned them there. And they took their bones and buried them under the tamarisk tree at Jabesh, and fasted seven days. (1 Samuel 31:11–13)

The men of Jabesh-gilead were heartbroken that their king had been exploited and their faith maligned. They spent seven days fasting and praying that the hurts would heal quickly.

The lesson of Saul's life has valid application to Christians today. We learn that a person who does not live in obedience to God is disqualified from living like a king, and will not have a kingdom that survives. Said another way, a life that is not lived in obedience to God

1) cannot be truly fulfilling,

2) cannot have lasting impact.

Disobedience does not nullify God's eternal grace to us, but it does interfere with His fullest blessing on our lives.

A person who chooses not to live in obedience to God cannot expect God to fight his spiritual battles for him, and defeat is inevitable. He can argue, scheme, cajole, or beg his way through a dilemma, and may achieve temporary victories, but defeat will eventually come. When defeat from the practice of disobedience is exposed, other people suffer as well. Families and close friends bear the brunt of the suffering, and hard-won territory is lost as Christian acquaintances face difficult questions and sometimes see their faith eroded. Rumors spread, reputations are devastated, churches split, and ministries are destroyed. The world does not miss an opportunity to proclaim the good news of the apparent failure of Christianity, as another fraud is exposed. Worse still, Christians in other communities and congregations agonize over how to respond to the way in which the name of God and His church are dragged through the mud or nailed to the wall.

Study Guide for Chapter 8

1. For content:
• Read 1 Samuel 13:1–14 and 1 Samuel 15.

• Why do you think it was so hard for Saul to admit that he had disobeyed God's commands?

• Saul's god was other people. What are some of the problems that occur when a person makes other people his god?

• Why is disobedience of God equated with witchcraft and divination? When we fail to follow God's directions, what are we following instead?

2. For further study:
• According to John 5:44, what happens when a person desires to get glory from other people rather than from God?

• How do people sometimes respond when they are caught doing the wrong thing? For example, what natural responses are mentioned in John 7:7; James 3:16; and James 4:1–2?

• Many of the commands of Jesus were quite simple to understand yet difficult to follow. For each of the following verses, give the simple meaning of the command and then list some of the excuses you may have heard or used as to why "He couldn't have meant that," or why "it doesn't apply in this situation" (Matthew 5:39–40, 42, 44; Matthew 6:19).

3. For application:
• Why is it difficult to admit when we disobey God's commands? Why is it difficult to see our own faults and yet so easy to see other people's faults?

• In what ways have you made other people your gods, and how does this affect your daily decisions?

4. For action:
• Make a list of excuses that you hear (or use) in one week. By comparison, how often do you hear acknowledgment of responsibility, such as a simple, "I was wrong"?

* Look up in a weekly newsmagazine the description of the failure of a well-known religious leader. What implications does the article make about the person, his associates, his followers, his beliefs, and his message?

5. For personal commitment:
3-by-5: Memorize 1 Samuel 15:22–23.

9.

Count Me Out

Genesis 14

"Just say no!" is a phrase that is showing up in many places these days. It is on billboards, bumper stickers, in magazines, and it represents the attempt to encourage kids to avoid involvement with drugs. I am not aware of any scientific studies on its effectiveness, but I fear that all this effort will have little real impact on the drug problem facing our nation.

The reason for my pessimism is that, as I understand human nature, it is next to impossible to "just say no." Peer pressure is too great, and the desire for acceptance too strong. For many kids, saying no to a friend or a peer means they will receive some form of ridicule or rejection that they are not strong enough to withstand for an extended period of time. The young man Daniel was unusual in his ability to stick to his convictions regarding what he would and would not eat, but he had the support of three like-minded friends who were praying for him and encouraging him.

The weakness of the "Just say no" campaign is that it is attempting to eliminate something without any suggestion of how to fill the hole that is left with something better and more meaningful. The fact is that our society does not have an adequate answer of how to replace drugs with something better.

Problems of this nature are not unique to the twentieth century. Nearly three thousand years before Christ, Abraham faced a situation where the temptation to compromise was strong, and yet, when he had thought about it, it was an offer he could refuse.

The problem arose when Lot and Abraham (then called Abram), returned from Egypt after an extended drought in Canaan to an area near Bethel. They had both accumulated so much wealth in livestock that it was not possible for them to live together. They had to separate, and Lot was given his choice of where to live.

Lot lifted up his eyes and saw all the valley of the Jordan, that it was well watered everywhere—this was before the LORD destroyed Sodom and Gomorrah—like the garden of the LORD, like the land of Egypt as you go to Zoar. (Genesis 13:10)

When Lot saw the valley of the Jordan, he was reminded of Egypt, and since life was so productive in Egypt, he decided this would be an ideal place for him. Throughout the Old Testament, Egypt is a symbol of living in the flesh, that is, pride in the human spirit and human strength. There are literally hundreds of warnings not to desire to live in Egypt or to go back to Egypt. Lot figured he could fear God yet live wherever he pleased, and this valley was the next best thing to Egypt. So Lot and his entourage moved into the cities of the valley of the Jordan, including Sodom.

We live in a nation of highly paid migrant workers. The typical timespan between transfers for many jobs is about three years, after which a family must sell their home and move to a new city, where they must find a new church, make new friends, and help children adjust to new schools. All of this is for what purpose? So that the career will advance and the salary will keep increasing. One wonders if it is really worthwhile to move to another city motivated by opportunities that are "just like in Egypt." Is the grass really greener somewhere else, and will my family do better there? Will my children be better behaved and less rebellious, and will I be better able to serve the

Christian community? Or is this move a well-disguised way to pretend to be serving the Lord while living as we please?

I remember when Bill decided a few years ago that he would not accept an offered promotion and transfer. By declining the offer, he jeopardized his job status. He could have been stranded on his rung of the career ladder, or worse, he could have lost his job, because he was not showing enough dedication to the company and its improvement. Because he had decided it was time for his family to settle down, he stuck to his guns. A short time ago, he was promoted to regional manager, without being required to move!

The move did not work out so well for Lot, and it was not long before the effects of Lot's compromise began to take its toll. The apostle Peter tells us that

Lot [was] *oppressed by the sensual conduct of unprincipled men (for by what he saw and heard that righteous man, while living among them, felt his righteous soul tormented day after day with their lawless deeds).* (2 Peter 2:7–8)

Lot had placed himself in an environment where he was in constant torment. He observed the people of the city doing things that he despised, he watched as their actions and attitudes influenced his family, he found himself gradually becoming like them, and there was nothing he could do to stop the erosion.

Because of his wealth, Lot also became involved, much to his dismay, in the political struggles of the area. At the time, there was a powerful king, named Chedorlaomer from Elam (modern-day Iraq in the Tigris and Euphrates valleys), who, together with an alliance of four other kings, dominated the regions of Babylonia and Canaan. For twelve years, the kings of the region of the valley of the Jordan (including those of Sodom and Gomorrah) were in servitude to Chedorlaomer, but after they rebelled, Chedorlaomer began a march to bring everyone back under his control. He marched (probably following the King's Highway to the east of the Jordan) to the south of the Salt Sea, conquering the cities of Kadesh-Barnea and Hazazon-Tamar (bordering the Negev wilderness on the Sinai Peninsula). On their return northward, they encountered the five regional kings in the valley of the Salt Sea. The text (Genesis 14:10) indicates that there were tar pits in the area, suggesting a source of fuel for the explosion and eruption that destroyed Sodom and Gomorrah, as well as Admah, Zeboiim, and Bela, some years later. This alliance of regional kings was soundly defeated, and as Chedorlaomer and his allies were collecting the spoils of war and food supplies from Sodom and Gomorrah, they captured Lot as well and took him with them.

When Abram learned this, he planned a rescue attempt.

When Abram heard that his relative had been taken captive, he led out his trained men, born in his house, three hundred and eighteen, and went in pursuit as far as Dan. (Genesis 14:14)

Even though Lot's decision to live in Sodom had led to this difficulty, Abram was prepared to come to his aid. He had not been able to dissuade Lot from making a bad decision, but he was still willing to come to Lot's rescue when he was in serious trouble.

It was typical at that time for a successful army to retreat to a safe distance and then have a victory celebration that lasted well into the night. Abram caught the army of Chedorlaomer completely off guard by attacking them at night, somewhere in the region of Damascus, about one hundred fifty miles from Sodom. Because the men of Chedorlaomer were probably stone-drunk, Abram was totally successful in rescuing Lot.

He brought back all the goods, and also brought back his relative Lot with his possessions, and also the women, and the people. (Genesis 14:16)

The return home was a great time of celebration. Abram was a hero, and, no doubt, enjoyed hearing the accolades of the released hostages.

He was elated over the totality of the victory, but at the same time, we know from Genesis 15:1, he was fearful of retaliation. At moments like this, it is tempting to accept offers that might be regretted later. It was very tempting to give Abram a handsome reward, and he deserved the honor. Sure enough, as they were coming back into the valley, the king of Sodom was there to greet Abram and make him an offer he couldn't refuse.

The king of Sodom said to Abram, "Give the people to me and take the goods for yourself." (Genesis 14:21)

In other words, "Abram, you can have all the spoils of this battle without any of the responsibilities. I'll take care of the physical and political needs of the people, but you can keep all the wealth."

Such an offer! All the wealth, none of the responsibility. But Abram declined.

Abram said to the king of Sodom, "I have sworn to the LORD God Most High, possessor of heaven and earth, that I will not take a thread or a sandal thong or anything that is yours, lest you say, 'I have made Abram rich.' (Genesis 14:22–23)

Abram saw within the offer of the king of Sodom a possibility for compromise. There was nothing externally wrong with the offer. It was common practice in those days for victorious leaders to keep the spoils of battle. In fact, Abram encouraged his men to take their fair share, as payment for their time and effort. But Abram knew that God had promised to make him great, and he wanted it to be clear to everyone that it was God who supplied all his needs, not the king of Sodom. He did not want to become indebted to the king of Sodom, so that the king of Sodom could at some later time use it as a lever to extract a favor. Abram's indebtedness was only to God, who never uses His gifts to us to extract favors later, and Abram wanted to keep it that way.

The offer made to Abram is not unlike the offers made by our society today. "Take the car now; nothing down and the seventy-two *easy* monthly payments do not begin for six months." "You can buy it now; just put it on the card." "Come on, take a drag. The buzz you get from it is great." But Abram declined.

What gave Abram the strength to resist such a tempting and apparently harmless offer? How was he able to decline the offer to have it all now?

The answer is hidden in three verses that we skipped over in the above recounting.

Melchizedek king of Salem brought out bread and wine; now he was a priest of God Most High. And he blessed him and said, "Blessed be Abram of God Most High, possessor of heaven and earth; and blessed be God Most High, who has delivered your enemies into your hand." And he [Abram] gave him a tenth of all. (Genesis 14:18–20)

On the way back from Damascus, Abram passed near Jerusalem (at that time known as Salem), through the Kidron Valley. As they passed by, Abram was met by Melchizedek, the king of Salem, and the two of them had a most important time together.

Very little is known about this mystery king, Melchizedek. He is mentioned in only two other places in the Bible, by David in a prophetic psalm about a coming priest and king,

The LORD has sworn and will not change His mind, "Thou art a priest forever according to the order of Melchizedek." (Psalm 110:4)

and by the writer of Hebrews (Hebrews 7), who explains much of the symbolism embodied in this person. His name means "the king is righteous," or "king of righteousness," and since Salem means "peaceful," he was "king of the peaceful city" or, "king of peace." His genealogy is not known, he simply appears and then is gone, with the sole purpose of his appearance to give a blessing to Abram.

It is striking that Melchizedek was "king of peace," "king of right-eousness," as well as priest of the Most High God. This is noteworthy because the Old Testament always kept the offices of priest and king separate. Recall that king Saul was strongly reprimanded (1 Samuel 13) when he took it upon himself to act as the high priest by offering a burnt offering. King Uzziah was confronted by the priests when he tried to enter the temple to burn incense (2 Chronicles 26). The prophet Zechariah knew that this combination was unusual when he foresaw the coming of a unique individual who would be both priest and king.

Yes, it is He who will build the temple of the LORD, and He who will bear the honor and sit and rule on His throne. Thus, He will be a priest on His throne, and the counsel of peace will be between the two offices. (Zechariah 6:13)

It is evident from this that Melchizedek is a picture of Jesus Christ, and that this encounter between Melchizedek and Abram is a picture of the ministry of Jesus to Christians.

The ministry of Melchizedek to Abram began with a meal, the similarity of which with the Christian sacrament of communion cannot be overlooked. It was served in the Kidron Valley, separating Jerusalem from the Mount of Olives, close to the site of the Garden of Gethsemane and the place in the Upper Room where Jesus would later serve the same ingredients to His disciples. It was a simple meal consisting of bread and wine. Bread pictures sustenance of physical need, and wine depicts sustenance of spiritual need. Indeed, this is exactly the message of Melchizedek, that God, because He is possessor of both heaven and earth, is able to satisfy Abram's every need, physical and spiritual. He can satisfy the need for food after a long tiring journey and hard battle, just as He can satisfy the spiritual needs for acclaim and acceptance and can calm fears of retaliation. "Abram, you can count on God to meet all of your physical and spiritual needs."

Jesus, in the ordinance of communion, expanded the meaning of the symbolism of the bread and wine. The bread became a symbol of

His own body that was broken for us, and the wine became a symbol of His blood that was shed for us. When Jesus said that His followers must eat His flesh and drink His blood (John 6:53), he was not suggesting cannibalism, but he was teaching that in Him one found sustenance for the body and for the spirit. Thus, the bread and the wine picture God's physical and spiritual provision for us, as well as our acceptance by God, because our sins are forgiven and our guilt before Him is removed.

What a blessing it is to belong to the One who owns and controls everything, and who has promised to take care of all your needs! In his role as priest, Melchizedek reminded Abram that he was accepted by God. Melchizedek, in his role as king, reminded Abram that God is the true king, and it is by Him that he was protected. There is no need to be king yourself; the job is already competently filled.

Notice how the phrases used in the blessing of Melchizedek made their way into the language of Abram. When he spoke to the king of Sodom, Abram repeated what he had been reminded of by Melchizedek, that he belonged to *"God Most High, possessor of heaven and earth."*

Abram's commitment to God was solidified by his gift to Melchizedek. Abram gave to Melchizedek a tenth of all the spoils. When we understand that God is the supplier of all things, it is easy to pass on to others the gifts that God has given us. It is no sacrifice to share with someone else that which has been generously given to us. There is no risk in freely giving to someone else when our needs are certain to be met. Indeed, a person who grasps selfishly to all that he has does not understand the generous provision of God.

"He is no fool who gives up what he cannot keep to gain what he cannot lose."—Jim Elliot

Early in my career I was faced with a decision of how I was going to order my life. I was hired into my first (untenured) academic job with other young men who were obviously dedicated to mathematical research. They seemed to work constantly. For example, it would often happen that if we discussed a problem at 5:00 one afternoon, they would have ten to fifteen pages of handwritten notes on the solution to the problem on my desk by 8:00 the next morning.

It is a common belief in academia that to get tenure, one must be a workahololic like these young men. It is almost like being an indentured slave, where the promise of tenure and academic freedom is offered to those willing to work hard enough for it.

During this time, I'd been asked to teach an adult Sunday school class at my church. Since I've had no formal theological or biblical training, I studied four nights a week to prepare for a forty-five-minute lesson. There was absolutely no way I could teach a Sunday school class and also work on mathematics for as many hours as my contemporaries. One Christian colleague warned me not to devote too much time to my Sunday school class because of the effect it might have on my career. The question that plagued and threatened me was whether I could be sufficiently productive in research to get tenure and a promotion when the standard was being set by brilliant young men who worked sixty to seventy hours a week. Or, because I devoted so much time to the study of the Bible, would I wash out of my career after my six-year probation period?

You know the answer, don't you? You see, God, who is possessor of heaven and earth, is able to present me with enough good ideas combined with efficiency and productivity to give me success in the career path He has chosen for me.

The lesson that we learn from the encounter of Abram with Melchizedek is just this: *There is nothing I need, whether it be a material possession or a spiritual boost, that God, through Jesus Christ, cannot provide.*

Whether it's physical or material, like cars and houses; or spiritual, like popular acclaim, acceptance, or relief from anxiety; the Lord God Most High is possessor of heaven and earth. He is able to deliver whatever I need into my hand.

Armed with the knowledge of what God has provided for me, through Jesus Christ, and that He offers these resources freely, I realize that anything the world can offer pales by comparison. I am not interested in other offers because I understand that they are not without consequences, and I don't need it, anyway. You see, my Father is "God Most High, possessor of heaven and earth."

Our country needs a new media campaign, encouraging people to "Just say yes!" Just say yes to the fact that we are sinners, in need of God's forgiveness and redemption; and just say yes to God's desire to provide for our every need. Then when we are faced with an offer from the world that seems "too good to refuse," we can look it squarely in the face and confidently say, "No thanks, you can count me out."

Study Guide for Chapter 9

1. For content:
• Read Genesis 14.

• What was the offer the king of Sodom made to Abram, and what was the hidden cost?

2. For further study:
• At the Last Supper, Jesus promised to care for the needs of his followers. Make a list of His promises as recorded in John 14.

• Why did the disciples (in John 6:60) have a hard time understanding what Jesus meant in John 6:51–57? Was Jesus suggesting cannibalism, or was He implying something else (John 6:63)? What did He mean? (John 6:35; 7:37–38)

3. For application:
• What are some of the offers that our society is making that are most tempting to you? What are the hidden costs of these offers?

• Write your own personalized paraphrase of Genesis 14:22–23.

4. For action:
• Write a short biographical sketch describing a person who made a decision without considering the hidden costs. It may be a person you know or one about whom you read in a newspaper or magazine.

5. For personal commitment:
3-by-5: Memorize Genesis 14:22–23.

Part III

Living a Life That Counts

He has told you, O man, what is good; and what does the LORD require of you, but to do justice, to love kindness, and to walk humbly with your God?—Micah 6:8

10.

Numbering My Days

Psalm 90:1–12

Three score and ten years is enough; if a man can't suffer all the misery he wants in that time, he must be numb.—Henry Wheeler Shaw, 1818–1885

There is something strange about us: we know we are going to die, but we often act as if we will live forever. I am in no hurry to die, and yet I must face the fact that my days are numbered.

Since his days are determined, the number of his months is with Thee, and his limits Thou hast set so that he cannot pass. (Job 14:5)

Moses also understood that his life was finite and going fast. Even though he lived to be e hundred twenty years old, and it was said of him at the time of his death that "his eye was not dim, nor his vigor abated," I suspect that he too was frustrated at times by the fact of his impending death. It was perhaps late in his career that he wrote Psalm 90 in which he expressed some universal feelings about life and death.

Thou dost turn man back into dust, and dost say, "Return, O children of men." For a thousand years in Thy sight are like yesterday when it passes by, or as a watch in the night. (Psalm 90:3–4)

I know a professor at Stanford University who worked out a mathematical theory for how to live as long as possible. The basic premise was that we each have been given a fixed number of heartbeats that we get to use up, and when they are gone, we die. The goal for this theory is to make the predetermined number of heartbeats last as long as possible. The problem, then, is to devise the most efficient exercise program, realizing that exercise uses up heartbeats at a fast rate, with the benefit that it lowers our heart rate when we are not exercising.

There are plenty of other schemes that attempt to lengthen life, but in the end, life seems pretty short. It seems like only yesterday that I was in college preparing for a career that now is more than half over. Life goes by so fast.

My sister Kathy died of cancer at age thirty-eight. What a terrible waste of a beautiful life! Yet, the fact is that, even though it is inevitable, death at any age is a terrible shame, a tragedy that goes against what *should* be. There is something inside each of us that makes us feel eternal, as if we should live forever. Aging or sickness ruin all that, and life ends long before it should.

Thou hast swept them away like a flood, they fall asleep; in the morning they are like grass which sprouts anew. In the morning it flourishes, and sprouts anew; towards evening it fades, and withers away. (Psalm 90:5–6)

Not only does life go by very fast, but it also seems that we accomplish so little that is of lasting impact. My best work, that which I was trained to do and worked so hard over, is either ignored or soon will be. Twenty years of education preparing for twenty years of hard labor are followed by twenty years of waiting for retirement.

There is no remembrance of earlier things; and also of the later things which will occur, there will be for them no remembrance among those who will come later still. (Ecclesiastes 1:11)

People want to be remembered. That is why towns, mountains, streets, and buildings are named after people. In academic professions, there are books that list the "important" people with a few lines of bibliography. I, along with most of my colleagues, have been invited at one time or another to have my name listed in *Who's Who in American Science.* Sounds impressive, doesn't it? What you probably didn't know is that to be listed in *Who's Who in American Science,* I would have to pay the publishers a substantial sum of money. Then, of course, I could purchase my own personal copy of the book for an appropriately reduced fee. You see, the biggest market for such a book is the people whose names are listed therein. The publisher is banking (literally) on the fact that people want to be remembered.

Life seems to be mostly a downhill skid.

We have been consumed by Thine anger, and by Thy wrath we have been dismayed. Thou hast placed our iniquities before Thee, our secret sins in the light of Thy presence. For all our days have declined in Thy fury; we have finished our years like a sigh. (Psalm 90:7–9)

"In like a lion, out like a lamb" is not only a description of the month of March, but also, quite often, of our lives. The vigor of youth is replaced by dotage, as our bodies are unable to keep up with our wishes. There is not much comfort in the fact that "you are never too old to yearn."

My life is about half over and already I am noticing the effects of age. I am simply not as fit or agile, either physically or mentally, as I was twenty years ago. I enjoy the joke that says that there are two signs of aging: The first is that you lose your memory, and the second is that you, well, uh, hmm, now what was I saying?

We live with the consequences of our mistakes, often for a long time. The consequences of a few mistakes can leave more damage than many good decisions can repair. One damaging car accident can leave more physical and emotional scars than hundreds of miles of safe driving can heal. One divorce can leave more hurts than years of happy marriage can heal. One illegitimate pregnancy can leave more bitterness than any number of legitimate babies can sweeten. Time is not a healer. Memories may fade with time; but time does not, it cannot, restore life that is lost.

There's really not very much to get excited about.

As for the days of our life, they contain seventy years, or if due to strength, eighty years, yet their pride is but labor and sorrow; for soon it is gone and we fly away. (Psalm 90:10)

With all of medical science at our disposal, we have not been able to lengthen our life expectancy beyond what it was in Moses' day. There have been periods of history during which, because of poor health care or diet, the life expectancy has dropped, and in Third World countries, the life expectancy is still low. All that medical research has been able to do is change the number one cause of death, and bring the life expectancy back to what it was 3,000 years ago. Scientists are completely baffled by the process of aging and cannot find ways to prevent it or slow it down.

Alas, there is not much that you or I can do to lengthen life.

Which of you by being anxious can add a single cubit to his life's span? (Matthew 6:27)

Exercise may help you stay healthy, but not much else.

Bodily discipline is only of little profit. (1 Timothy 4:8)

Not only is it impossible to lengthen one's life, but our achievements are hard-won and transitory. Someone was asked at the time of J. D. Rockefeller's death how much he had left behind. The answer,

"All of it," was to the point. Some people think that "he who dies with the most toys wins," but he takes with him exactly the same as everyone else. Solomon expressed this same frustration.

As he had come naked from his mother's womb, so will he return as he came. He will take nothing from the fruit of his labor that he can carry in his hand. . . . Exactly as a man is born, thus will he die. (Ecclesiastes 5:15–16)

Perhaps more disappointing is that our hard-won accomplishments provide little lasting satisfaction even while one is alive.

I considered all my activities which my hands had done and the labor which I had exerted, and behold all was vanity and striving after wind and there was no profit under the sun. (Ecclesiastes 2:11)

Our life is short, full of struggles, and quickly forgotten. Furthermore, it is sometimes hard to understand what God is doing, why He allows certain things to happen and why, at times, He seems so angry.

Who understands the power of Thine anger, and Thy fury, according to the fear that is due Thee? (Psalm 90:11)

Do you get the impression that Moses was having a bad day when he wrote Psalm 90? With this downcast outlook on life, one wonders what kind of advice Moses has for us. If this is the way things are, how should we then live?

Teach us to number our days, that we may present to Thee a heart of wisdom. (Psalm 90:12)

Do you catch the significance of what Moses is saying? "You can't take it with you," refers to your body and your material possessions.

But there is something we *do* take with us, namely, our spiritual wisdom.

Unfortunately, this translation of Psalm 90:12 is not completely accurate. In the Hebrew text, the indirect object *to Thee* is not present, and the verb *present* is perhaps better translated "bring in." The term is of agricultural origins, meaning that we bring in, or harvest, or store up wisdom in a storehouse. But the command to store something up so that we will have it in the future is found in other Scriptures as well.

Do not lay up for yourselves treasures upon earth, where moth and rust destroy, and where thieves break in and steal. But lay up for yourselves treasures in heaven, where neither moth nor rust destroys, and where thieves do not break in or steal. (Matthew 6:19–20)

So the idea of Moses' statement is that we are to store up wisdom, which no one can take away from us, so that when we die and leave this earth, we have a ready basis for our continuing relationship with God.

Growing old does not guarantee that we grow wise. There are probably as many old fools as there are young fools. Perhaps you have known people, as I have, who, the more teeth they lose, the more biting they get.

But Paul's perspective is that the most important feature of aging is our spiritual growth, not our physical deterioration.

We do not lose heart, but though our outer man is decaying, yet our inner man is being renewed day by day. (2 Corinthians 4:16)

Our outer man is finite, but our inner man is eternal. Only what is done for the inner man has any lasting effect. Don't fight aging; fight foolishness!

What does it mean to number our days? Certainly it does not mean that we should count backwards, starting at some predetermined number and marking days off a calendar until we reach zero, at which time we will die. Exact information regarding how long you or I will live is not available. Rather, numbering our days means that we should not waste our time doing useless things, but that we should come to a correct understanding of the true meaning of life. Then, with this understanding, we make good use of the time available to us to become spiritually wise, and in doing so, to build our relationship with God.

I would summarize the advice of Scripture on how to number our days with four specific statements:

1) Adopt a long-term view.

Ezra had a long-term view of his life and where he was going.

Ezra had set his heart to study the law of the LORD, and to practice it, and to teach His statutes and ordinances in Israel. (Ezra 7:10)

That is, Ezra had predetermined that his life was to be characterized by the disciplines of study, practice, and teaching of God's Word. From his spiritual disciplines, other aspects of his life would take their direction. I imagine that there were some days when one or more of these things failed to get done, but over the long haul, there was a consistency about his life that was characterized by these disciplines. We too should see that there is a long-term plan in operation in our lives.

While I was writing this book, there were days when I was sure it was a total waste of time. I remember one day in particular when I received yet another rejection letter. I had to remind myself to keep an eternal perspective about this project, remembering that the delays that can be so frustrating to me are inconsequential to God. He is neither surprised nor is His plan for me upset by these things.

I am confident of this very thing, that He who began a good work in you will perfect it until the day of Christ Jesus. (Philippians 1:6)

The apostle Paul's long-term view can be summarized as follows:

I bow my knees before the Father . . . that He would grant you, according to the riches of His glory, to be strengthened with power through His Spirit in the inner man. (Ephesians 3:14–16)

Okay, Paul, so what does it mean to be strengthened in the inner man?

So that [1] *Christ may dwell in your hearts through faith; and* [2] *that you, being rooted and grounded in love, may be able to comprehend with all the saints what is the breadth and length and height and depth, and to know the love of Christ which surpasses knowledge,* [3] *that you may be filled up to all the fulness of God.* (Ephesians 3:17–19)

In other words, we become strengthened in the inner man when we become filled to overflowing with the knowledge of God and His love. When this happens, there are no gaps or holes, and no reasons to be fooled into thinking that the gods of this world have something to offer that God cannot provide. We realize that the deepest pleasures of life are found when we are living in relationship with God. We understand that we fulfill our purpose when we glorify God by enjoying Him forever. Ezra would tell us to fill our lives with things that help us to know God through His Word and to live in response to that.

2) Aggressively move beyond failure and accept change.

One of the biggest obstacles to progress is the reminder of failure. Paul would never let past failures become an obstacle to new attempts.

Not that I have already obtained it, or have already become perfect, but I press on in order that I may lay hold of that for which also I was laid hold of by Christ Jesus. Brethren, I do not regard myself as having laid hold of it yet; but one thing I do: forgetting what lies behind and reaching forward to what lies ahead, I press on toward the goal for the prize of the upward call of God in Christ Jesus. (Philippians 3:12–14)

Notice Paul's intensity and passion here. Paul was not willing to become comfortable with the status quo, but desired to be constantly challenged and growing, in spite of obstacles and setbacks. The growing Christian is one who is not bored but is mentally and spiritually alert, committed to the spiritual disciplines, studying the Bible, reading good books, writing poems, prayers, and songs, praying with intensity for God's leading, and teaching others. It is necessary to have your mind challenged and your spirit shaped by new ideas and new ways of doing things. Notice the importance of the mind and the spirit in bringing about change in the following verses:

Do not be conformed to this world, but be transformed by the renewing of your mind. (Romans 12:2)

. . . that you be renewed in the spirit of your mind. (Ephesians 4:23)

Gird your minds for action, keep sober in spirit. (1 Peter 1:13)

We dare not become complacent and satisfied with where we are spiritually, nor allow old habits and hurts to bog us down. We must not dwell on the bitterness of the past, such as an abusive parent or a substandard education, or use them as excuses for why we are spiritually stagnant now. Instead, we must forgive and move on.

Let us also lay aside every encumbrance, and the sin which so easily entangles us, and let us run with endurance the race that is set before us. (Hebrews 12:1)

3) Have a short-term plan.

In other words, set daily disciplines, and monthly or yearly goals and objectives that help you move in the direction God is leading you. With each day, have an idea of what you want to accomplish that day.

Do you not know that those who run in a race all run, but only one receives the prize? Run in such a way that you may win. And everyone who competes in the games exercises self-control in all things. . . . Therefore I run in such a way, as not without aim. (1 Corinthians 9:24–26)

Solid food is for the mature, who because of practice have their senses trained to discern good and evil. (Hebrews 5:14)

Recall that Ezra desired to practice what he learned, and according to Paul (2 Timothy 3:16), Scripture is profitable, not just for teaching (i.e., knowledge), but also for *training.* Our training comes as we develop spiritual disciplines such as meditation, prayer, fasting, worship, and service. The apostle Peter (2 Peter 1:5–6) tells us that our disciplines should promote diligence, moral excellence, knowledge, self-control, perseverance, godliness, brotherly kindness, and love.

We accomplish big goals one day at a time. Place yourself in situations or find activities wherein these desired character traits are developed gradually out of necessity. For example, to develop knowledge, have a regular pattern of reading. To read one book this month, schedule to read a few pages every day. To develop brotherly love, spend an hour a week serving food at a rescue mission. To develop diligence and perseverance, lead a Bible study or teach a children's Sunday school class for a predetermined length of time. But remember the warning of Moses (Deuteronomy 7:22) that victories come little by little, not all at once. It may take years to get control over a temper or an attitude of laziness, but without practice and spiritual discipline, there is no hope for change.

4) Keep track of your progress

As you set and meet goals, make note of it (in a journal, perhaps) so that your progress is apparent.

Take pains with these things; be absorbed in them, so that your progress may be evident to all. (1 Timothy 4:15)

It is especially important that you have some help in sticking to your goals and in recognizing when progress is being made. For this, Scripture recommends that we be accountable to someone who will encourage us when we are discouraged and will be brutally honest when we are impressed with ourselves.

Two are better than one because they have a good return for their labor. For if either of them falls, the one will lift up his companion. But woe to the one who falls when there is not another to lift him up. And if one can overpower him who is alone, two can resist him. A cord of three strands is not quickly torn. (Ecclesiastes 4:9–10, 12)

You need to have one or two genuine friends to help you stay on track. For over ten years I have met weekly for breakfast with Bob. We have been through a lot together. He has prodded me on when I have wanted to run and hide, and I have encouraged him when the load he was carrying got very heavy.

What is it that you want to present to God when you stand before Him? What goals have you established for your inner person? What specific steps are you taking to move in that direction? Moses would encourage us to number our days so that we can present to God a heart that is full of wisdom. We number our days when we

1) know our purpose and keep an eternal focus,

2) remain motivated to accept change,

3) have a plan that involves specific actions,

4) keep ourselves accountable to other wise people.

The tragedy of many people is that while they plan for their retirement, they do not plan for eternity. Eternity is a certainty, retirement is not. They try to grow rich in money, but do not grow rich in wisdom, not realizing that wisdom is the treasure you take with you. Their goals for wisdom are either nonexistent or set very low. The sad fact is that *if you aim for nothing, that is exactly what you will hit!*

What a nice epitaph to have for one's gravestone: "He was rich in wisdom, and he took it all with him." So, Lord, teach us to number our days that we may present to you a heart of wisdom.

Study Guide for Chapter 10

1. For content:
• Read Psalm 90:1–12.

• Write in your own words what it means to have a strong inner person.

2. For further study:
• According to 1 Timothy 6:18–19, how do we store up a treasure for the future?

• What weaknesses of the inner person were exposed by the actions described in Mark 9:31–34, 38 and John 9:18–23?

• What does Hebrews 12:15 imply about old hurts and memories?

• According to Philippians 1:6, on what basis can we adopt a long-term view for life?

• Make a list of at least six reasons from 2 Corinthians 4:13–18 of why we do not lose heart.

3. For application:
• What are specific goals for your Christian growth for the next year? What specific actions are you taking to help meet those goals?

• What is your criteria for a good day? That is, when someone asks you, "Did you have a good day?" what things lead you to say "yes" and what things lead you to say "no"?

4. For action:
• Everyone knows ways to fight aging—(even though they don't work!). Make a list of ways to fight foolishness.

5. For personal commitment:

10-for-10: For the next ten days, take ten minutes each day to read and meditate on the suggested passage, and record your thoughts and ideas about the passage in your journal. For each day when a new passage is suggested, be sure to review the previous day's passage first.

Days 1–2: Psalm 90

Days 3–4: Proverbs 3:1–12

Days 5–6: 2 Peter 1:3–11

Days 7–8: Ephesians 3:14–21

Days 9–10: 1 Corinthians 9:24–27; Philippians 3:12–16

11.

Making My Life Count

Psalm 90:13–17

I can't get no satisfaction, I can't get no daily action, cause I've tried and I've tried and I've tried and I've tried.—Mick Jagger

According to trend analysts, yuppieism is dead. It took about a decade, but the change occurred as yuppies began to take inventory of their lives. They found food processors, pasta makers, expresso makers, exercise machines, hot tubs, portable telephones, answering machines, fax machines, laptop computers, and remote controls for the television, the VCR, the CD player, the stereo receiver, and the garage door opener, but they did not find satisfaction. It seems that they have finally discovered the truth of the old maxim that you cannot buy happiness. They were trying to find some meaning in their lives and were not finding it in department stores.

Everyone would like to know that life has significance, or more specifically, that one's own life is significant, and that what he or she is doing is worthwhile. We each measure our worth in different ways. Many people measure their significance by their job promotions and pay raises. In scientific circles, the coveted phrase is that "his work made a significant contribution to . . . ."

For some, fame is a measure of significance. If a mathematician's name is recognized by 10,000 or more other mathematicians, he is considered "famous" and therefore significant. An interesting exercise is to determine what gives different people a feeling of significance. For example, what is it that gives a sense of significance to doctors, homemakers, actors, lawyers, carpenters, assembly-line workers, professional athletes, or truck drivers?

I was surprised when I first realized that Moses struggled with this same problem. Moses, who confronted Pharaoh, and led the descendants of Jacob (renamed Israel) out of slavery in Egypt, founded a nation that still exists today. Imagine Moses, who was perhaps the greatest political leader of all time, whose contributions impacted the legal system, the economic system, the military, the agriculture, and the social welfare system of that foundling nation, struggled to know that his life had significance!

In Psalm 90:13–17, Moses wrote,

"Do return, O LORD; how long will it be? And be sorry for Thy servants. O satisfy us in the morning with Thy lovingkindness, that we may sing for joy and be glad all our days. Make us glad according to the days Thou hast afflicted us, and the years that we have seen evil. Let Thy work appear to Thy servants, and Thy majesty to their children. And let the favor of the LORD our God be upon us; and do confirm for us the work of our hands; yes, confirm the work of our hands."

Life is hard, and then you die, or so it seems when you look at all of the difficulty in the world. Moses recognized that life is hard, and that there are some mornings, like Monday morning, when it is hard to get up and get going. Perhaps Moses was not a morning person, but wouldn't it be nice, he asks, if he could wake up every morning with a satisfied feeling coming from the realization of God's love for him?

Maybe you get up in the morning singing praises to God, full of the assurance that God loves you and that what you are about to do is significant. If so, you are of rare character. The rest of us need help in this area.

Moses makes two requests of God that should help us. His first request is this: *Let Thy work appear to Thy servants, and Thy majesty to their children.*

In other words, we need to see how awesome and majestic God is, and we need to see that He is at work in the world.

Most of the people I work with are atheists, or if not atheistic, feel very little need for God. If you ask a person on the street what God has been doing in the world or in their own life, you would be met with an incredulous stare as if you, not they, are out of touch with reality. To most people, if God is not dead, then He is certainly taking an extended holiday.

The problem is that while the acts of God are seen by everyone, not everyone is willing to attribute them to God. As Romans 1:20 says, while

His invisible attributes, His eternal power and divine nature, have been clearly seen, being understood through what has been made,

people are unwilling to honor God as God. Everyone marvels at the devastating power of a tornado or the awesome wonder of newborn life, yet there are a variety of explanations for these events. "It happened by chance" seems to work for some people. Many scientists try to explain everything by the "laws of nature," thinking that the world is a big complicated machine governed by these laws of nature, so that if all the data for the present were known, one could predict exactly what would happen in the future. This view of the world ignores two important facts: First, the spiritual nature of humankind, and second, the unpredictability of deterministic systems.

People are spiritual beings, restrained, but not determined by the laws of nature. We are not chemical automata. There is something extra operating inside a person that goes beyond chemistry and physics, that cannot be described or predicted on the basis of the laws of nature.

I believe that one manifestation of the spiritual realm is creativity, or the emergence of ideas. Because ideas cannot be generated at will, I believe that the thinking of a good idea is a supernatural event, a miracle, if you wish. To be sure, ideas can be suppressed, and they are restrained by the laws of nature; but ideas are not produced by a law of nature, they belong to the realm of spiritual activity.

As long as people have ideas, the future of the world cannot be predicted. I observe God at work as He changes and directs the minds and attitudes of people.

Even if everything were governed by the laws of nature, that is not enough to know the future. Mathematicians have recently discovered that many things are deterministic, but not predictable. Something is deterministic when the law governing its motion is known, and if one knew exactly its state now, its future states could be calculated exactly. However, because I am a finite being, I can never know anything exactly. For example, no one knows, *nor can it be known*, the exact value of π (the ratio of a circle's circumference to its diameter). The exact value of π involves an infinite number of digits, and I can at best determine a finite number of them in a finite lifetime (which is all I have available).

The problem with "chaotic" deterministic systems is that even the smallest error in the initial data eventually leads to errors in the calculation in which all information of the past is lost. That is, two calculations, starting with data that are arbitrarily close together, ultimately lead to states or motions that have no relationship to each other whatsoever. In meteorology, this is called the "butterfly effect," as the erratic flight of a butterfly in Southeast Asia can change the effect of a snowstorm in the Rocky Mountains. Even with perfect understanding of the laws of nature, finite beings cannot predict the future with accuracy. As long as we are finite, we cannot predict the future of the natural world.

Now, when someone comes along who uses with certainty the timing of a "natural" event to his advantage, we can conclude that it was a lucky guess, or that it was known in advance. If it was known in advance, only an infinite God could have known it. For example, consider the timing of a wind storm to coincide with the Israelites' desperate need to cross the Red Sea (Exodus 14), the timing of an earthquake-induced landslide to block the Jordan River at Adam, so the Israelites could cross the Jordan River at Gilgal (Joshua 3), the timing of an earthquake so that the walls of Jericho collapsed (Joshua 6), the timing of a flash flood in the valley of Megiddo so that Sisera's army was washed up (Judges 4), or the timing of a rainstorm after three-and-one-half years of drought to coincide with Elijah's consuming fire on Mount Carmel (1 Kings 18). Even with the best of scientific knowledge, the timing of events like these cannot be predicted by finite men. Equally significant, many of the political events of the nation of Israel, such as the Assyrian and Babylonian conquests, were predicted before they occurred (Isaiah 8; Habakkuk 1), but they could not have been predicted by the best of political scientists.

In spite of all the best arguments, some people are still not convinced that God is in control of the natural world or that God is at work in the lives of people. Many eyewitnesses were not convinced by Jesus' miracles that He was as He claimed, "come from God." This is because while the acts of God are clearly visible, His majesty and greatness must be revealed, and this is why Moses makes the request that God allow Himself to be seen. He says something similar in Deuteronomy 3:24:

O Lord GOD, Thou hast begun to show Thy servant Thy greatness and Thy strong hand; for what god is there in heaven or on earth who can do such works and mighty acts as Thine?

Moses was over a hundred years old when he wrote this. In other words, it took a while, but eventually Moses began to see God's greatness and His power to act. But the point is this: We also need to come to understand that God is at work in the world and in the lives of people.

It is true that God must reveal Himself to us, but we can make it easier for Him! Take a walk in the woods, or in the desert, and observe the miracle of life. Look at the incredible variety and intricacies of patterns and marvel at the process of reproduction. Take a good descriptive biology course and learn to see the incredible wonders of God's handiwork. Then take a descriptive geology course and begin to observe the awesome forces that it took to push up the mountains and carve the valleys and create the lava cones. Read a book on astronomy or walk in the desert at night and gaze at the heavens and the amazing size of the universe, with its seemingly uncountable stars and planets.

Next, learn about atomic physics and atoms and molecules and quarks, and try to figure out what holds protons together, and what is the nature of the gravitational force. If that is not enough, take a course in molecular biology to learn about the structure and function of DNA, and the enormous amount of genetic information that is packed into tiny spaces. Or you could study physiology to see the amazing complexity of the human body and marvel that everything actually works. If you really want to be baffled, take a psychology course to realize that essentially nothing is known about how the mind works, or what constitutes thinking or memory. For that matter we do not know what constitutes life. I could go on and on. You can never run out of things to discover about the works of an infinite God.

Great are the works of the LORD; They are studied by all who delight in them. Splendid and majestic is His work. (Psalm 111:2–3)

When I consider Thy heavens, the work of Thy fingers, the moon and the stars, which Thou hast ordained; what is man that Thou dost take thought of him? And the son of man, that Thou dost care for him? (Psalm 8:3–4)

As we begin to see God's majesty, we further understand that there is significance and purpose to what is going on around us. We are part of a magnificent display of creative power. Life has significance; there is a design behind it, a purpose for it, and it is leading somewhere.

Just as Moses first asked God, "Let Thy work appear to Thy servants, and Thy majesty to their children," the second part of Moses' request for significance is this: *Let the favor of the LORD our God be upon us; and do confirm for us the work of our hands.*

Once we see that God is at work in the world and in the course of human history, we also desire to know that we personally play a significant role in that plan. We need confirmation that our own work is worthwhile and is fitting with the purpose of life. Surely you want to know that your career is more significant than the gold watch you receive at retirement. I know I do.

How can our work be confirmed? Moses addresses this question in his writings when he mentions "the work of our hands." Let's look at his advice.

You shall again obey the LORD, and observe all His commandments which I command you today. Then the LORD your God will prosper you abundantly in all the work of your hand. (Deuteronomy 30:8–9a)

The first way to be assured that what you do is significant is to place your *highest priority on obeying God.*

It is abundantly clear from Scripture that God designed you for a special reason.

Join with me in suffering for the gospel according to the power of God; who has saved us, and called us with a holy calling, not according to our works, but according to His own purpose and grace which was granted us in Christ Jesus from all eternity. (2 Timothy 1:8–9)

We are His workmanship, created in Christ Jesus for good works, which God prepared beforehand, that we should walk in them. (Ephesians 2:10)

Do you remember the encouragement the young man Jeremiah received when he was called to be a prophet?

Before I formed you in the womb I knew you, and before you were born I consecrated you; I have appointed you a prophet to the nations. (Jeremiah 1:5)

If God knows for what purpose He designed us, it only makes sense that the most fulfilling way to live is to follow that plan and be obedient to God.

His divine power has granted to us everything *pertaining to life and godliness, through the true knowledge of Him who called us by His own glory and excellence. For by these He has granted to us His precious and magnificent promises, in order that by them you might become partakers of the divine nature, having escaped the corruption that is in the world by lust.*

Now for this very reason also, applying all diligence, in your faith supply moral excellence, and in your moral excellence, knowledge; and in your knowledge, self-control, and in your self-control, perseverance, and in your perseverance, godliness; and in your godliness, brotherly kindness, and in your brotherly kindness, Christian love. For if these qualities are yours and are increasing, they render you neither useless nor unfruitful in the true knowledge of our Lord Jesus Christ. For he who lacks these qualities is blind or short-sighted, having forgotten his purification from his former sins. Therefore, brethren, be all the more diligent to make certain about His calling and choosing you; for as long as you practice these things, you will never stumble. (2 Peter 1:3–10; emphasis mine)

The phrase *make certain* in the last verse is a bit confusing. It could be taken to mean that Peter wants us to do everything in our power to make sure that God chooses us. Picture a first-grade student who knows the answer to his teacher's question, jumping up and down, waving his hand, hoping the teacher will pick him this time. This is not what Peter means. There is nothing we can do to coax God into choosing us. Instead, we must understand that Peter wants us to *become* certain, that is, to become reassured by getting to know God better, that we are called by God. As we are reassured and confident that God has called us and chosen us, we come to the firm conclusion that there is no better way to live than in obedience to Him. A life lived in obedience to God is *neither useless nor unfruitful.*

The second instruction of Moses about fulfillment is as follows:

At the end of every third year you shall bring out all the tithe of your produce in that year, and shall deposit it in your town. And the Levite, because he has no portion or inheritance among you, and the alien, the orphan and the widow who are in your town, shall come and eat and be satisfied, in order that the LORD your God may bless you in all the work of your hand which you do. (Deuteronomy 14:28–29)

When you reap your harvest in your field and have forgotten a sheaf in the field, you shall not go back to get it; it shall be for the alien, for the orphan, and for the widow, in order that the LORD your God may bless you in all the work of your hands. (Deuteronomy 24:19)

In other words, if we want to have blessing and affirmation in what we do, we must make it a high priority to *care for the needs of others.* This points out a basic fact of the human psyche, that there is tremendous personal satisfaction in knowing that what one does is of benefit to someone else. In fact, because we were created for good works (Ephesians 2:10; 2 Timothy 3:17), we find satisfaction in doing what we were designed for. God gives us pleasure when we help meet the needs of someone else.

There are many jobs in our society where this perspective has been lost, and this loss is unfortunate. Many scientists are driven by the desire to show other people how clever they are. Many business-people are driven by the desire to make lots of money, so that profitability becomes more important than product safety, air quality, or customer satisfaction. The tragedy is that many people have lost the sense that what they do is, or should be, of benefit to someone else. Jesus encouraged His followers to become servants of others with the

full understanding that in so doing we receive a deep sense of job satisfaction. Moses' advice to us today would include the encouragement
to overcome the drudgery of our jobs by finding new ways, or putting
new emphasis on old ways, that the needs of others are served.

The final word of instruction from Moses on confirmation is,

*Seven days you shall celebrate a feast to the LORD your God in the
place which the LORD chooses, because the LORD your God will bless
you in all your produce and in all the work of your hands, so that you
shall be altogether joyful.* (Deuteronomy 16:15)

Moses said that in order to put the final cap of confirmation on
what you are doing with your life, to be altogether joyful, you should
have a big celebration honoring God. Have a party! Take time to sing,
eat, play games, and laugh with your extended Christian family, in celebration and gratitude for all the great things that God does for us.
Make worship of God serious business, not serious in the sense of
somber, but serious in the sense that it is done with gusto and intensity.
The deepest joy you will ever experience is in genuine worship of
God. When we finally get serious about praising and honoring God for
all that He has done, we become altogether joyful, and confirmed in
who we are and what we are doing.

There it is. Moses' instruction on how to find fulfillment from
the work He has given you to do. It begins as God reveals himself to
us through His works and His majesty. We then come to understand
that we are important to God and play a significant role in what He is
doing as we

1) make obedience to God our highest priority,
2) place a high priority on serving others,
3) get serious about worshiping God.

There is one summarizing piece of advice about confirming the
works of our hands.

The LORD your God has blessed you in all that you have done.
(Deuteronomy 2:7)

The LORD will open for you His good storehouse, the heavens, to give rain to your land in its season and to bless the work of your hand. (Deuteronomy 28:12)

Simply stated, *God is the One who blesses us.* We deserve no credit for anything good that comes our way. If we fail to recognize God as the source of all blessing, we jeopardize our confirmation. Everything we are is a gift from God, whether it is athletic ability, intellectual prowess, or financial acumen. If you want to fully enjoy the gifts you have been given, give credit where credit is due.

Study Guide for Chapter 11

1. For content:
• Read Psalm 90:13–17.

• People who feel insignificant often make poor decisions about their relationships, choosing to participate in abusive and degrading relationships or activities. Why?

• Write out your own paraphrase of 2 Peter 1:3–10.

2. For further study:
• According to Deuteronomy 29:29, there are some things about God that simply cannot be known. Can you think of some? What is the point of those things about God that have been revealed?

• According to Ephesians 2:10 and 2 Timothy 3:17, what are Christians created for?

• How does the Bible define fruitfulness? See, for example, Galatians 5:22–23 and Ephesians 5:8–10.

• On what basis does Jeremiah (in Jeremiah 30:18–19) say that a person is not insignificant?

• According to John 4:34, what gave Jesus true satisfaction and a sense of accomplishment?

3. For application:
• How have you seen the splendor and majesty of God recently?

• From what do you derive your greatest satisfaction at your place of employment? Are there ways you might modify your goals to improve your level of satisfaction?

• Who are the aliens, orphans, and widows in your community? What are some of their needs that you can meet?

• Using 2 Peter 1:3–10, list some specific activities that will make you fruitful and useful.

4. For action:
• This week do at least two of the following for "aliens, orphans, and widows."
- Baby-sit for a young couple or parents of a handicapped child so that they can go out for coffee.
- Call an elderly person on the phone just to talk.
- Take a child from a broken family on an outing (hiking, biking).
- Tutor an international student in English.
- Pray with a friend on the steps of an abortion clinic for the young mothers who are struggling with their decision regarding an unwanted pregnancy.
- Invite a new couple or family to go out to dinner with your family after church.
- Take your children to visit with other children at the local shelter for homeless families.
- Take an elderly person shopping or for a drive in the country.
- Send a note of encouragement to a college student living away from home.
- Bake some cookies or buy some bagels for someone in your Bible study.
- Do something different and then add it to this list.

* Read an article in *Scientific American* and then tell someone what you learned about the splendor of God from the article.

5. For personal commitment:
3-by-5: Memorize 2 Peter 1:8.

12.

A Life That Didn't Add Up

1 Kings 10–11

It seems that whenever I go to a professional meeting or a conference, I meet a person who appears to have it "all together." He or she is well-groomed, well-spoken, self-assured, accompanied by a "knockout" traveling companion, admired by outside observers, and apparently in need of nothing. Often, however, upon further scrutiny, serious deficiencies in their life that are hidden from the view of the general public become apparent.

My friend, Butch, recently met someone like this. He is the CEO of a successful company that he founded, is monetarily set for life, and by his own admission, he has "done it all." Yet in private conversation over coffee he admitted to Butch that his life is empty and meaningless.

How does this happen? How is it that a person with enormous talent and energy can end up feeling that his life does not count for much, or that his accomplishments are not fulfilling? Where did he go wrong?

King Solomon was a very impressive person. He was incredibly wealthy, probably ten times as wealthy as his father, David, and his fame was widespread. No hero of antiquity, with the possible exception of Alexander the Great, is more celebrated in folk literature.

We learn something of how impressive a man he was from his encounter with the queen of Sheba.

When the queen of Sheba heard about the fame of Solomon concerning the name of the LORD, she came to test him with difficult questions. (1 Kings 10:1)

The queen of Sheba was curious to learn what kind of person Solomon was, and she was also interested in maintaining friendly trade relations with him. Solomon controlled the trade routes through Palestine, while the queen of Sheba controlled trade routes from India and Africa through the Arabian cities of Mecca, Medina, and Tema.

She came to Jerusalem with a very large retinue, with camels carrying spices and very much gold and precious stones. (1 Kings 10:2)

Solomon was apparently personable, because the queen had no difficulty opening up to him.

When she came to Solomon, she spoke with him about all that was in her heart. (1 Kings 10:2b)

Solomon is always described as being a wise man, but he was also clever and quick-witted. Legend has it that he and Hiram, the king of Tyre, regularly challenged each other with riddles for the other to solve. He also had insight into human nature, as reflected by many of his collected proverbs.

God gave Solomon wisdom and very great discernment and breadth of mind, like the sand that is on the seashore. And Solomon's wisdom surpassed the wisdom of all the sons of the east and all the wisdom of Egypt. For he was wiser than all men, than Ethan the Ezrahite, Heman, Calcol and Darda, the sons of Mahol; and his fame was known in all the surrounding nations. He also spoke 3,000 proverbs, and his songs were 1,005. (1 Kings 4:29–32)

The queen of Sheba was not able to stump him with any of her questions.

Solomon answered all her questions; nothing was hidden from the king which he did not explain to her. (1 Kings 10:3)

The queen was also impressed with Solomon's house. It took seven years for Solomon to build the temple, and thirteen years to build his own house. Both were impressive structures. You can read a description of the house in 1 Kings 7. We are told in 1 Kings 5, that Solomon used 30,000 men to haul raw materials from Lebanon, 80,000 men to cut stone, and 70,000 men to transport cut stone from the mountains; there is no mention of how many additional people were needed for the actual construction of these buildings.

The queen of Sheba also noticed the quantity and quality of the food necessary to keep his household running. One day's provision included 300 bushels of flour, 600 bushels of meal, 10 fat (barn-raised) oxen, 20 pasture-fed oxen, 100 sheep, as well as deer, gazelles, and fowl (1 Kings 4:22–23).

Solomon's house was a masterpiece of organization. He had servants, waiters, cupbearers—all exquisitely dressed and in the right place at the right time.

Solomon knew how to run a business and was indescribably wealthy. He had a fleet of ships based in the southern port of Ezion-Geber which brought all kinds of exotic goods, such as monkeys, parrots, gold, ivory, sandalwood, and various precious stones to Israel. There was so much silver in Jerusalem at the time that it was considered nearly worthless.

He was an importer and breeder of fine horses, had 1,400 chariots, and kept 12,000 horsemen. Since Solomon never went to war, his horses and chariots were used mostly for racing.

What the queen of Sheba saw was so impressive that it left her exhausted and overwhelmed. His reputation had not prepared her adequately for what she saw and experienced. But her visit to King

Solomon was apparently an economic and political success, because we are told

King Solomon gave to the queen of Sheba all her desire which she requested. (1 Kings 10:13)

This desire may have included sexual intimacy, because according to Ethiopian legend, recorded in the *Kebra Nagast* ("Glory of the Kings"), she later gave birth to the first king of Ethiopia, fathered by Solomon. Haile Selassie, emperor of Ethiopia from 1930 to 1974, claimed to be a descendant of that union.

As she left the palace, one of her summarizing statements was

"How blessed are your men, how blessed are these your servants who stand before you continually and hear your wisdom." (1 Kings 10:8)

In other words, "What a neat place to live! It must be wonderful living with you in your home."

Was his home a wonderful place to live? Was Solomon a wonderful person to be around? Did what the queen of Sheba saw in this brief visit coincide with the internal reality of Solomon's life?

The truth is that with all of his wisdom, possessions, organizational skill, and accomplishments, Solomon was a miserable man. Furthermore, his accomplishments are pretty much forgotten in the subsequent biblical record. His name is mentioned twenty-three times outside of the books of Kings and Chronicles, and these are usually in reference to something that is better than Solomon, or referring to something that Solomon built. Solomon, the man, is not held up as someone to emulate. All the wealth that he had accumulated and the kingdom that he had built began to fall apart immediately upon his death.

Even though he apparently had everything a man could possibly want, it did not satisfy him. He denied himself nothing, and yet he concluded that it was all in vain.

All that my eyes desired I did not refuse them. I did not withhold my heart from any pleasure, for my heart was pleased because of all my labor and this was my reward for all my labor. (Ecclesiastes 2:10)

In other words, Solomon treated himself well, because, after all, he told himself, "I'm worth it."

I considered all my activities which my hands had done and the labor which I had exerted, and behold all was vanity and striving after wind and there was no profit under the sun. (Ecclesiastes 2:11)

Even though he thought himself deserving of the "good things" in life, those things did not satisfy him. His hard work and accomplishments were not enough, and left him empty, still looking for something else.

Among the other things that Solomon pursued were women. He had three hundred wives and seven hundred concubines. There was not a sexual fantasy that he could not pursue, yet these were not satisfying to him. His physical desires were totally out of control. Josephus wrote that Solomon "grew mad in his love of women, and laid no restraints on himself in his lusts." While some of his marriages solidified political alliances and probably involved only minimal sexual contact, the fact remains that among his wives he did not have a devoted friend or trusted confidante. I don't imagine that he asked any of his wives to proofread his writings, for if he had, they certainly would have been disheartened by his admission that

I have found one man among a thousand, but I have not found a woman among all these. (Ecclesiastes 7:28)

Solomon had a full head but an empty heart. Just as his interpersonal relationships did not provide true satisfaction, so too his religious practices showed that he was searching for something that he was unable to find.

It came about when Solomon was old, his wives turned his heart away after other gods; and his heart was not wholly devoted to the LORD his God, as the heart of David his father had been. For Solomon went after Ashtoreth the goddess of the Sidonians and after Milcom the detestable idol of the Ammonites. And Solomon did what was evil in the sight of the LORD, and did not follow the LORD fully, as David his father had done. Then Solomon built a high place for Chemosh the detestable idol of Moab, on the mountain which is east of Jerusalem, and for Molech the detestable idol of the sons of Ammon. (1 Kings 11:4–7)

Ashtoreth was a sex goddess of the Sidonians; and Milcom, Chemosh, and Molech are described as detestable because they were gods to whom children were offered as burnt sacrifices. (The mountain east of Jerusalem, where Solomon built a high place for Chemosh, is the Mount of Olives.) Solomon's religious pursuits were a reflection of his private thought life, and they were disgusting and detestable.

Not only was Solomon not pleased by his wives or their gods, neither was Solomon able to please them. He was driven by and constantly reminded of their demands.

Thus also he did for all his foreign wives, who burned incense and sacrificed to their gods. (1 Kings 11:8)

He was constantly building altars for his wives so that they could worship their own gods as they wanted. I imagine their living quarters were filled with the smells of incense and burnt flesh. His wives got whatever they wanted, but it was never enough. A man's home is supposed to be his palace, but this was a man who had a palace that was not his home.

Was it a pleasure, as the queen of Sheba had opined, to be a servant in his house? Apparently not.

Jeroboam the son of Nebat, an Ephraimite of Zeradah, Solomon's servant, whose mother's name was Zeruah, a widow, also rebelled

against the king. Now this is the reason why he rebelled against the
king: Solomon built the Millo, and closed up the breach of the city of
his father David. (1 Kings 11:26–27)

The reason for the rebellion in Solomon's household is not apparent from this description. The problem related to Solomon's building
program. In order to build the temple and his palace he had required
the labor of large numbers of slaves (taken from the Amorites, Hittites,
Perizzites, Hivites, and Jebusites who were descendants of inhabitants
of Canaan before the conquest) and numerous conscripted Israelite laborers. The construction of the temple and his palace took twenty
years, and I imagine that during that time he reassured the Israelite laborers that they would be free to pursue other endeavors as soon as all
this construction was finished. Furthermore, there was an enormous
bureaucracy that had built up around Solomon, the maintenance of
which placed an onerous tax burden on the people. After Solomon's
death, the first request the people made of Rehoboam, Solomon's son
and heir to the throne, was that this burden be lightened.

Early in his reign, Solomon married the daughter of the pharaoh
of Egypt in order to form a political alliance, and during the initial
stages of the building program, she lived in temporary quarters. When
the palace was finally finished, she was not happy and demanded that
an additional wing be added to the palace for herself. Then, when her
wing of the palace was finished, she demanded that an old Jebusite cit-
adel, called the Millo, be rebuilt.

Israelites were supposed to be free people, and after the Exodus
from Egypt they had been continually warned not to desire to return
to the slavery of Egypt. But here they were, in their own land, in
forced servitude to the whims of an Egyptian princess and numerous
other foreign women. This was too much to take, and rebellion erupt-
ed, led by Jeroboam, a young industrious supervisor over some of Solomon's forced laborers.

So here we see Solomon as a man who had done it all and was still
miserable. To the outside observer he was pleasant, witty, organized,

successful, good company; but in reality, he had a perverted thought life, an empty soul, a drivenness to please wives who did not please him. A despotic man to work for.

What went wrong? Why did Solomon's life count for so little?

A clue to what went wrong in Solomon's life is found in the writings of Moses. In Deuteronomy 17, Moses describes the kind of person that should be selected to serve as the king of Israel.

"You shall surely set a king over you whom the LORD your God chooses, one from among your countrymen you shall set as king over yourselves; you may not put a foreigner over yourselves who is not your countryman. Moreover, he shall not multiply horses for himself, nor shall he cause the people to return to Egypt to multiply horses, since the LORD has said to you, 'You shall never again return that way.' Neither shall he multiply wives for himself, lest his heart turn away; nor shall he greatly increase silver and gold for himself. Now it shall come about when he sits on the throne of his kingdom, he shall write for himself a copy of this law on a scroll in the presence of the Levitical priests. And it shall be with him, and he shall read it all the days of his life, that he may learn to fear the LORD his God, by carefully observing all the words of this law and these statutes, that his heart may not be lifted up above his countrymen and that he may not turn aside from the commandment, to the right or the left; in order that he and his sons may continue long in his kingdom in the midst of Israel." (Deuteronomy 17:15–20)

According to Moses, the king should be chosen from among the people, a commoner, if you please, so that "his heart would not be elevated above his countrymen." He was not to be a foreigner, because a foreigner would not relate well to the needs of the people.

He was not to be a person who desired to have many horses or who encouraged people to return to Egypt to acquire horses. Horses, especially Egyptian horses, were a symbol of physical power, and the king was to be a person who relied on the Spirit of God to fight his battles, not the physical power of horses, chariots, and horsemen.

The king was supposed to be a person who did not accumulate wives or gold and silver for himself. The warning against wives was because they could perhaps turn his heart away from God. Quite simply, with many wives to take care of and relate to, there would be too many demands to give adequate attention to one's own relationship with God.

I live in a state where polygamy was once legal and is still practiced openly. Frankly, I have enough difficulty being a good husband and father with one family. I can't imagine the increased stress with more.

More problematic, an accumulation of wives shows that the king does not believe that a relationship with God is adequate to fill all of his needs. He may marry for political convenience or for physical pleasure, but in either case it is a statement that God does not know how to take care of his physical needs. Similarly, a heavy reliance on the accumulation of gold and silver shows that the man does not believe that God is adequate to provide for his material needs.

Solomon did all three of these proscribed things. He imported Egyptian horses and chariots, had numerous wives, and collected vast amounts of silver and gold, in direct defiance of an explicit command. But as we read on, we see a further problem.

The king should be a person who pays significant attention to God's Word, by writing it out, by reading it, by letting it permeate him, and by carefully observing what it says. The king is supposed to be a person who lives by the Book.

There was nothing inherently wrong in Solomon's composition of poems and clever proverbs, or in the collection and compilation of the works of clever people around him. Of much higher importance should have been that he write, in his own hand, an exact copy, verified by the Levitical priests, of God's law. This exact copy of the law was to be his daily guidebook, so thoroughly imprinted on his mind and heart that he never deviated from obedience to its commands. But you can see from his writings and his collections of proverbs that the writings of Moses had little influence on him.

Unfortunately, Solomon was a man whose highest priority in life was not his relationship and obedience to God.

On two occasions, God appeared to Solomon with an appeal that he make obedience of God his highest priority. The first appearance was early in Solomon's reign, shortly after he had married the pharaoh's daughter. It was Solomon's practice to offer sacrifices and burn incense at the high places. The high places were altars left over from religious practices of pagan Canaanite nations, and there was a great high place in Gibeon, at which Solomon offered a thousand burnt offerings. He was not supposed to be offering sacrifices at the high place in Gibeon, since the only acceptable place for sacrifices was at the ark of the covenant, which currently resided in Jerusalem.

It was in demonstration of His grace that God appeared to Solomon in a dream at Gibeon.

In Gibeon the LORD *appeared to Solomon in a dream at night; and God said, "Ask what you wish me to give you."* (1 Kings 3:5)

This is the stuff of which fairy tales are made, like the genie in Aladdin's lamp, by whom three wishes are to be granted. But notice the importance of this question. "Solomon, what do you want out of life, and how can I provide it for you?"

How would you answer this question? If you had exactly one request you could make of God, what would you ask for? What is the most important thing that God can do for you?

Solomon's request was not terrible.

Give Thy servant an understanding heart to judge Thy people to discern between good and evil. For who is able to judge this great people of Thine? (1 Kings 3:9)

God did not criticize Solomon for his request, because he could have done worse. He could have asked for something blatantly selfish, like long life or wealth or victory over his enemies, but he didn't. God honored his request by promising him wisdom, as well as things he did not ask for, such as wealth and fame. But on closer inspection of Solomon's request, we can see his primary motivation.

Solomon said, "Thou hast shown great lovingkindness to Thy servant David my father, according as he walked before Thee in truth and righteousness and uprightness of heart toward Thee; and Thou hast reserved for him this great lovingkindness, that Thou hast given him a son to sit on his throne, as it is this day. And now, O LORD my God, Thou hast made Thy servant king in place of my father David, yet I am but a little child; I do not know how to go out or come in. And Thy servant is in the midst of Thy people which Thou hast chosen, a great people who cannot be numbered or counted for multitude" (1 Kings 3:6–8)

Solomon recognized that his father David was a special man whose heart was strongly committed to God. David had a relationship with God that was exemplary. Solomon felt inadequate to take over from such a man as David. He felt that because of his age and inexperience, he was unskilled in king-like protocol and might embarrass himself following such a great man as his father. He was worried about how he looked. He recognized that he was to govern an impressive group of people, and he felt intimidated by it all. So his request is essentially that he be a good king, a good leader of the people, and that he have a good reputation with them, and not make a fool of himself.

This is analogous to my wanting to be a good mathematician, or a good professor; or for your wanting to be a good doctor, a good banker, a good bus driver, or a good parent. There are people who have needs to be met, and we want to be proficient in serving their needs, and we want to be well-liked and recognized for doing a good job.

But there is a better choice. Notice that Solomon did not say anything at all about becoming like his father, or having a relationship with God that was like that of his father. Solomon wanted to be a good king, but his relationship with God took a lower priority. God nudges him in this better direction at the end of His response with the words

If you walk in My ways, keeping My statutes and commandments, as your father David walked, then I will prolong your days. (1 Kings 3:14)

God tried a second time, some twenty years later, to get through to Solomon with essentially the same reminder, after

Solomon had finished building the house of the LORD, and the king's house, and all that Solomon desired to do. (1 Kings 9:1).

Perhaps now that he had done it all, he would recognize the void in his life and make a personal commitment to God, but there is no recorded response from Solomon.

There are other examples of distorted priorities. Recall the words of Jesus to Martha when she was busily serving food and drink while Mary sat at the feet of Jesus, listening to His words.

"Martha, Martha, you are worried and bothered about so many things; but only a few things are necessary, really only one, for Mary has chosen the good part, which shall not be taken away from her." (Luke 10:41–42)

Mary had chosen to build a relationship with Jesus, and Martha had decided to be of service to others. Mary made the best choice; Martha could have chosen better.

Consider the admonition to the church at Ephesus.

"'I know your deeds and your toil and perseverance, and that you cannot endure evil men, and that you put to the test those who call themselves apostles, and they are not, and you found them to be false; and you have perseverance and have endured for My name's sake and have not grown weary. But I have this against you, that you have left your first love.'" (Revelation 2:2–4)

The church at Ephesus consisted of people who placed a high priority on doctrinal accuracy and exposing false teachers, but they had grown cold and hypocritical and no longer had an emphasis on maintaining a relationship with God. The warning to them is that "I will remove your lampstand out of its place," that is, their impact on other people's lives would disappear unless they first reordered their priorities.

According to Jesus, the two most important commandments are, in this order, to love God, and to love your neighbor as yourself (Matthew 22:36–40). Service to others is important, but it is secondary to having a loving, obedient, relationship with God. The wisdom that Solomon requested was the wisdom he needed to be a good king and to serve his nation well. But there is a higher wisdom, a wisdom that teaches us how to order our personal lives and how to live in loving obedience to God. We are choosing poorly when we choose to place Christ's second commandment ahead of His first.

In contrast to Solomon, the most important thing to David was his relationship with God.

One thing I have asked from the LORD, that I shall seek: that I may dwell in the house of the LORD all the days of my life, to behold the beauty of the LORD, and to meditate in His temple. (Psalm 27:4)

The apostle Paul used different words, but expressed the same idea.

[I pray] *that He would grant you, according to the riches of His glory, to be strengthened with power through His Spirit in the inner man; so that Christ may dwell in your hearts through faith; and that you, being rooted and grounded in love, may be able to comprehend with all the saints what is the breadth and length and height and depth, and to know the love of Christ which surpasses knowledge, that you may be filled up to all the fulness of God.* (Ephesians 3:16–19)

[I desire] *that their hearts may be encouraged, having been knit together in love, and attaining to all the wealth that comes from the full assurance of understanding, resulting in a true knowledge of God's mystery, that is Christ Himself, in whom are hidden all the treasures of wisdom and knowledge.* (Colossians 2:2–3)

Paul recognized, as did David, that the most important wisdom we can have is a wisdom that helps us to know, and to be filled up with, and to be passionately consumed with, the love of God. There is no higher or more fulfilling wisdom. There is no more rewarding way to live.

Moses was right. If you want to live a life that counts for something, make it your highest priority to have a loving, obedient relationship with God. What the world needs is not better lawyers, judges, economists, teachers, plumbers, computer programmers, or CEOs. The world needs more people who have a full understanding of the glory and majesty of Almighty God, and whose highest priority is to know and obey the living God. My prayer for Butch's friend, as for other "successful" people of the world, is that he would commit his life to Christ, allowing Him to be his Lord, who alone can bring fulfillment and purpose to an empty life that is full of things that don't add up.

Study Guide for Chapter 12

1. For content:
• Read 1 Kings 10–11.

• Summarize Solomon's external appearance and the internal reality of his life.

• What mention is made of Solomon in the New Testament? See, for example, Matthew 6:29 and Luke 11:31.

• Why did Moses (in Deuteronomy 17:14–20) recommend that the king of Israel not seek to have numerous wives, riches, and horses?

2. For further study:
• Find five things in the book of Ecclesiastes 1 and 2 that frustrated Solomon. How are Solomon's frustrations evident in our society? How do the words of Jesus in John 6:27 pinpoint the source of the difficulty?

• What priorities are expressed in John 5:44 and John 12:42–43, and what actions do these effect?

• How is it that apparently good activities can become distractions? How does Luke 10:38–42 illustrate this?

3. For application:
• Where do people in our society derive their highest sense of purpose, meaning and satisfaction? Are these an adequate basis for life or, if not, why are they inadequate?

• Not all choices are the same; some are better than others. What are some of the better choices mentioned in Psalm 69:30, Psalm 84:10, and Hosea 6:6, and how should they influence our actions?

• If you had one wish for your life, what would it be? (Honestly?)

4. For action:
• Interview three different people (preferably non-Christians) to determine their short-term and long-term goals and to ascertain where they find their deepest sense of satisfaction and fulfillment. What do they want to get better at and why? Be sure to ask the question asked of Solomon, "If you could have exactly one wish for your life, what would it be?"

5. For personal commitment:
3-by-5: Memorize Psalm 27:4.

13.

Living Like a King

1 Samuel 9

"How would you like to be Queen for a Day?" With these words and to the applause of the audience, the host of the popular fifties television show "Queen for a Day" started the process by which some lucky lady chosen from the studio audience would be showered with gifts beyond her wildest dreams. I have a friend who won a complete set of kitchen appliances as a participant on a television game show. What a lucky lady!

I also have a number of friends who have received MacArthur Fellowships, tax-free grants of about $300,000 to be used for any purpose, no strings attached. I must admit that when I learned of their good fortune, I jealously wished I had been chosen for the same honor.

Perhaps you would prefer to win the Publisher's Clearing House sweepstakes or the lottery in your state. So how would you react if, out of the blue, you were selected to be a king or a queen?

As a matter of fact, if you are a Christian, you have been chosen to live the life of a king. In Romans 8, we are told that because we have been adopted into God's family, we are heirs of the kingdom of God, and therefore fellow heirs with Jesus Christ. We are children of the King of kings, and He wants us to live like it.

Since we have been selected to live like kings, it would be worthwhile to figure out what it means to live like a king. Does it mean I
will live like Prince Charles, running around the world making public
appearances, or like Louis XIV, holding absolute political power?

The biblical perspective on how a king should live is different
from the common world-view, just as living in the kingdom of God is
different from life in the kingdom of the world. When King Shishak
of Egypt attacked Judah, the prophet Shemaiah explained to Rehoboam, king of Judah, the reason some of his people would be captured.

*They will become his slaves so that they may learn the difference
between My service and the service of the kingdoms of the countries.*
(2 Chronicles 12:8)

Because the differences are vast, we too need to learn the difference between living like a king in God's kingdom and living like a
king in the world.

We have already seen from Deuteronomy 17 the type of person
who was to be king. He was to be an ordinary person from their own
country who would not feel the need to be elevated above the rest of
the people. He was to be a person who did not seek to build a large
defense industry, a large household of wives, or a vast storehouse of
wealth. He was to be a person who knew and loved God's Word.

So what is the point of being a king with all these restrictions? After all, isn't it the goal to become powerful with lots of servants, to be
fabulously wealthy, to have all of my fantasies fulfilled, and to be
above the law rather than subject to it?

The two advantages to being a king are *freedom* and *opportunity*.
There is freedom from routine tasks that can fill a day. There is freedom from the clock; the king does not punch a clock. The advantage
I have of being a salaried rather than an hourly worker is that I am
free to work when conditions are best. I often work late at night after
my children are in bed, and I would prefer to skip Monday mornings

altogether. For a king, there is freedom to make decisions, and not be entangled by rules or expectations that may hinder his work.

With increased freedom comes increased opportunity to do things of significance. Because his own needs are attended to, there is opportunity to attend to the needs of others. The prophet Jeremiah reminded Shallum, who became king of Judah following Josiah, his father, that being a king means more than having the fanciest home.

"Woe to him who builds his house without righteousness and his upper rooms without justice, who uses his neighbor's services without pay and does not give him his wages, who says, 'I will build myself a roomy house with spacious upper rooms, and cut out its windows, paneling it with cedar and painting it bright red.' Do you become a king because you are competing in cedar? Did not your father eat and drink, and do justice and righteousness? Then it was well with him. He pled the cause of the afflicted and needy; Then it was well. Is this not what it means to know Me?" declares the LORD. (Jeremiah 22:13–16)

In today's society, many people think they are living like kings if their multistory homes are trimmed in oak with teal accents, rather than as in Shallum's day with cedar trimmed in red. The color scheme has changed, but the issue is the same; being able to compete in oak does not make you a king. A hot tub or a wide-screen TV in a recreation room with a wet bar or a heated garage containing late-model luxury cars does not mean you are living like a king. You become a king when your relationship with God gives you the freedom to see beyond your own needs, and to recognize and serve the needs of other people around you.

Although he did not follow his own advice, King Solomon described the heart of a good king in Psalm 72.

Give the king Thy judgments, O God, and Thy righteousness to the king's son. May he judge Thy people with righteousness, and Thine afflicted with justice. Let the mountains bring peace to the people, and the hills in righteousness. May he vindicate the afflicted of the people, save the children of the needy, and crush the oppressor. (Psalm 72:1–4)

He will deliver the needy when he cries for help, the afflicted also, and him who has no helper. He will have compassion on the poor and needy, and the lives of the needy he will save. He will rescue their life from oppression and violence; and their blood will be precious in his sight. (Psalm 72:12–14)

Dewey was the financially successful manager of a popular fast-food restaurant, but his restaurant was running his life, with long hours and lots of pressure, with the consequence that his family and his relationships with other Christians suffered. One day he was reminded of Paul's description of Jesus.

Have this attitude in yourselves which was also in Christ Jesus, who, although He existed in the form of God, did not regard equality with God a thing to be grasped, but emptied Himself, taking the form of a bond-servant, and being made in the likeness of men. And being found in appearance as a man, He humbled Himself by becoming obedient to the point of death, even death on a cross. (Philippians 2:5–8)

Dewey knew what he had to do when he wrote in his notebook his own paraphrase of these verses as follows:

Jesus took a lower paying job in order to spend more quality time with His family.

Dewey recognized that a king uses his financial freedom to take advantage of opportunities to be of service to others. He quit his job at the restaurant and started a Christian bookstore in which he hired family members and Christian friends, and developed discipleship programs through his store that served both employees and customers.

So it should be with us. We should see that God has given us freedom to pursue opportunities to be of service to others, and in this service we find that our lives count for something significant.

Perhaps you do not feel that you are living like a king, but you feel a bit like Saul before he became king of Israel.

There was a man of Benjamin whose name was Kish . . . . And he had a son whose name was Saul, a choice and handsome man, and there was not a more handsome person than he among the sons of Israel; from his shoulders and up he was taller than any of the people. Now the donkeys of Kish, Saul's father, were lost. So Kish said to his son Saul, "Take now with you one of the servants, and arise, go search for the donkeys." And he passed through the hill country of Ephraim and passed through the land of Shalishah, but they did not find them. Then they passed through the land of Shaalim, but they were not there. Then he passed through the land of the Benjamites, but they did not find them. (1 Samuel 9:1–4)

Saul was a striking young man with great potential. Although he did not know it at the time, he was destined to be king of Israel, but when we first meet him, he is chasing donkeys. In his culture, donkeys were an important beast of burden. They could carry heavy burdens or be ridden, or be used to plow fields and trample seed into the ground. But donkeys could also be stubborn, and as Saul learned, elusive and frustrating.

Do you feel like you spend much of your time chasing donkeys? The donkeys in your life are the things that might be nice to have, admired by your culture, but they are elusive, stubborn, and often produce frustration. Perhaps it is a longed-for job promotion, recognition, or honor. It might be a home in an upscale neighborhood, or a red sports car. If you are single, it may be a relationship with a special person that you wish would lead to marriage but so far has gone nowhere. Usually it is some area of self-interest that nags at us and the more we chase it, the more our frustration mounts. Paying attention to donkeys diverts attention away from more important things.

Saul cannot be faulted for chasing donkeys. He was simply doing what his father had asked of him, and what his culture demanded. He had no idea that God had a different plan for him.

As the search dragged on with no success, and he was running out of supplies and money, Saul decided to call off the search and return home, so that his father would not become concerned for his safety. Saul's servant, however, had another suggestion.

"Behold now, there is a man of God in this city, and the man is held in honor; all that he says surely comes true. Now let us go there, perhaps he can tell us about our journey on which we have set out." (1 Samuel 9:6)

The frustration of the donkeys provided the occasion for Saul and his servant to seek godly advice. Had he not been led on this "wild donkey chase" around the countryside, he would not have been near Samuel's home. If he had found the donkeys first, he would have gone home without visiting Samuel.

Yet Saul objected to visiting Samuel. If Samuel was a man of God, then Saul should give him a gift, but they were out of food and money, and he had no gift for the man. His servant told Saul not to worry, he could cover it.

"I have in my hand a fourth of a shekel of silver; I will give it to the man of God and he will tell us our way." (1 Samuel 9:8)

Not knowing exactly where to go, Saul and his servant stopped a woman on the outskirts of the city to ask for directions on how to find this man of God. "Is the seer here?" they asked.

"He is; see, he is ahead of you. Hurry now, for he has come into the city today, for the people have a sacrifice on the high place today." (1 Samuel 9:12)

Samuel was an itinerant prophet who had arrived in the city a few minutes before Saul and his servant. As Saul entered the city he saw a man walking toward the high place, so he stopped the man and asked for directions to the prophet's house. The man responded, "I am the prophet."

What a coincidence! Saul and the servant just happened to be led by the donkeys into the vicinity of Samuel's hometown. The servant (not known for financial independence) just happened to have squirreled away some money that he was willing to let Saul use as a gift to Samuel. Samuel just happened to have arrived in town a few minutes before Saul and his servant, and walking down the street, they just happened to bump into the very man they were looking for.

This was no coincidence, but instead God had arranged a meeting of significance. God does the same thing today.

Fred was a student of mine who upon completion of his Ph.D. had a number of options open for his future and was seeking God's leading. He was trying to decide between an academic career in the West or the life of a missionary to Moslems in Central Asia. Although he had accepted a job for the coming academic year at Oxford University, he'd spent the summer following his thesis defense traveling to a number of places around the world to assess the opportunities and to ascertain God's leading.

During his travels he came twice to Salt Lake City, both times with the hope that we could spend time discussing God's leading in his life. We played various rounds of phone tag, trying to find a way to spend some time together, but to no avail. I was also traveling, and our paths simply did not cross. Late in the summer, I went to a professional meeting in Bristol, England, and decided to spend an extra day in Oxford, touring the countryside on a bicycle and visiting with colleagues. In the early evening I returned my rented bicycle to the rental shop, and was walking back to my room at the bed-and-breakfast near the train station, when a tap on my shoulder was accompanied by "Hi!" It was Fred.

We spent the next five hours eating pizza, going to a concert, and talking about God's leading in his life. I learned then that Fred was spending four weeks near London, and had decided to visit Oxford for one day to survey the possibilities of renting an apartment before his move there later in the fall. Fred had never been to Oxford before, and did not know ahead of time that I would be there.

You see, when God wishes to arrange a meeting between people, He can make it happen.

Samuel had been prepared by God for his meeting with Saul, and he answered Saul's questions before Saul even had a chance to ask them.

"Go up before me to the high place, for you shall eat with me to-day; and in the morning I will let you go, and will tell you all that is on your mind. And as for your donkeys which were lost three days ago, do not set your mind on them, for they have been found. And for whom is all that is desirable in Israel? Is it not for you and for all your father's household?" (1 Samuel 9:19–20)

Without being asked, Samuel took care of Saul's immediate needs. He invited Saul to dinner and told Saul not to worry about the donkeys because they had been found. He then added a cryptic remark about some special blessing for Saul and his family, leaving Saul completely confused. At dinner that night Samuel placed Saul at the head of the table and gave him a special portion of meat, reserved for an honored guest.

Early the next morning, Samuel woke Saul to send him on his way home. As they were walking down the street toward the edge of town, Samuel told Saul about his future.

Samuel took the flask of oil, poured it on his head, kissed him and said, "Has not the LORD anointed you ruler over His inheritance?" (1 Samuel 10:1)

In other words, Samuel announced to Saul that he had been chosen to be king of Israel. Then he told Saul what to expect in the coming days.

"When you go from me today, then you will find two men close to Rachel's tomb in the territory of Benjamin at Zelzah; and they will say to you, 'The donkeys which you went to look for have been found. Now behold, your father has ceased to be concerned about the donkeys and is anxious for you, saying, "What shall I do about my son?"' Then you will go on further from there, and you will come as far as the oak of Tabor, and there three men going up to God at Bethel will meet you, one carrying three kids, another carrying three loaves of bread, and another carrying a jug of wine; and they will greet you and give you two loaves of bread, which you will accept from their hand. Afterward you will come to the hill of God where the Philistine garrison is; and it shall be as soon as you have come there to the city, that you will meet a group of prophets coming down from the high place with harp, tambourine, flute, and a lyre before them, and they will be prophesying. Then the Spirit of the LORD will come upon you mightily, and you shall prophesy with them and be changed into another man." (1 Samuel 10:2–6)

Samuel promised Saul that three things would happen to him. First, someone would meet him and confirm that the donkeys had been found and were no longer a matter of concern. Second, he would meet three men who would provide him with food, and finally, God's Spirit would come upon him and he would be a changed man, empowered by His Spirit to proclaim God's Word.

The application for Christians today is *exactly* the same. We have been adopted into God's family and have been anointed to be heirs of God's kingdom. Furthermore, through Christ,

1) we have been freed from chasing donkeys.

I do not know what your most frustrating donkey is, but whatever it is, you do not need to be chasing it. God has a better plan for you.

Since we have so great a cloud of witnesses surrounding us, let us also lay aside every encumbrance, and the sin which so easily entangles us, and let us run with endurance the race that is set before us. (Hebrews 12:1)

or in a crude paraphrase, "Let us quit chasing the donkeys in our lives and get on with the business of living like kings."

2) God has given us freedom from anxiety about our daily existence.

He has promised to provide for all of our needs.

"I say to you, do not be anxious for your life, as to what you shall eat, or what you shall drink; nor for your body, as to what you shall put on. Is not life more than food, and the body than clothing?" (Matthew 6:25)

"Do not be anxious then, saying, 'What shall we eat?' or 'What shall we drink?' or 'With what shall we clothe ourselves?' For all these things the Gentiles eagerly seek; for your heavenly Father knows that you need all these things. But seek first His kingdom and His righteousness; and all these things shall be added to you." (Matthew 6:31–33)

3) God has freed us from inability,

because through His Spirit He has gifted us in some special way for some special task that is useful in the service of God's kingdom (Romans 12:6; Ephesians 3:7).

Since Christ has freed us from chasing donkeys, freed us from daily concerns, and given us the gift of God's Spirit enabling us to do some special task, we are free to pursue opportunities of service. It is in this way that Christ has enabled us to live like kings, and to know that our lives count for something eternal when we do.

It is as if God is the announcer on stage asking you and me the question, "How would you like to be king for a lifetime?" But first you have to stop chasing the donkeys.

Study Guide for Chapter 13

1. For content:
• Read 1 Samuel 9–10.

• What three things were promised to Saul in 1 Samuel 10:2–6?

2. For further study:
• What are some of the characteristics of adoption into God's family? (Add to or comment on the following list)
    a) It is permanent (John 10:27–29),
    b) it is personal (Romans 8:14–17),
    c) it is a privilege (Galatians 4:4–7).

• Read Ephesians 1:3–6. How does adoption make us free?

• What were the people of Israel chasing after in their search for a king? (1 Samuel 8:4–6, 19–20; 9:2). How would you characterize the criteria we apply for the selection of our political leaders?

3. For application:
• What are the most significant distractions in your life that keep you from enjoying your relationship with God?

• How does being adopted into the family of God affect your priorities, your decisions, and your actions regarding the things you chase after?

• Perhaps you see your life as filled with menial tasks. In what sense do they also give you freedom and opportunity? How can you live like a king when you work like a servant?

4. For action:
• The meanings of adoption, parenthood, and child custody are being reevaluated by our society and in our courts. Find the description of a

recent incident in which these issues were in the limelight (for example, a child "divorcing" parents, natural parents suing to overturn an adoption, a surrogate mother wanting her child back). Compare adoption in this context with adoption into God's family and reflect on how these differences might affect the adoptee.

* Read *The Practice of the Presence of God* by Brother Lawrence.

5. For personal commitment:
3-by-5: Make a personal commitment to rid yourself of one donkey (from the application above) by keeping a description of the distraction on a 3" x 5" card in a prominent place and by committing it to God in prayer every morning this week.

14.

The Blessing and the Curse

Deuteronomy 8

I have never been one to dislike wealth. If God wants to bless me with money, I see no reason to stop Him. In fact, I rather like being blessed, and I figure it is a whole lot better than the alternative. I see no good reason why I should not be blessed, and I appreciate the question of Tevye from *Fiddler on the Roof* when he asks, "Would it spoil some vast eternal plan, if I were a wealthy man?"

There are some people who think that if they pray and have enough faith God will automatically bless them with health and wealth. These members of the "Health and Wealth Club" reason that if they are not wealthy or healthy, their weak faith is to blame.

Other people who are well-to-do or healthy figure that it is because, after all, they deserve it. "He is a self-made man and he worships his maker" says it fairly well.

The truth is that life consists of both difficulty and blessing, and God is the author of it all. Moses helps us understand this in Deuteronomy 8.

"All the commandments that I am commanding you today you shall be careful to do, that you may live and multiply, and go in and possess the land which the LORD swore to give to your forefathers." (Deuteronomy 8:1)

Moses wanted us to know that there are three excellent reasons to live in obedience to God: that we may live, multiply, and possess our inheritance. A life lived in obedience to God is lived to the fullest, is fruitful, and experiences full possession and enjoyment of its inheritance; that is, it is a life that counts for something. But life doesn't always seem that way. There are times when life is difficult, when life is a desert or a wilderness. What should be learned from our wilderness experiences?

"You shall remember all the way which the LORD your God has led you in the wilderness these forty years, that He might humble you, testing you, to know what was in your heart, whether you would keep His commandments or not. And He humbled you and let you be hungry, and fed you with manna which you did not know, nor did your fathers know, that He might make you understand that man does not live by bread alone, but man lives by everything that proceeds out of the mouth of the LORD. Your clothing did not wear out on you, nor did your foot swell these forty years. Thus you shall know in your heart that the LORD your God was disciplining you just as a man disciplines his son." (Deuteronomy 8:2–5)

Never forget your wilderness experiences! Their purpose is to test your character, to see what kind of person you really are, and to reveal, not only to God, but to yourself as well, what your heart is like. Are you thoroughly committed to a life of obedience, or do you live in obedience to God only when things are going well, and when God's leadership is in directions you already want to go?

God tests us by seeing how well we react to humiliation. Most of us want to be in charge of our life and figure that we can run it quite well, thank you. It is humbling for us to find out that we are incapable of providing anything for ourselves, and that everything we have and are is a gift from God. We experience humility when God lets us go hungry, either for physical or spiritual food, because then we discover that we cannot provide for ourselves, and our inability is exposed for all to see. Sometimes we lose our jobs and do not know where the grocery money or next month's rent will come from. At other times we are faced with questions that we cannot answer, problems that we cannot solve, broken relationships that we cannot mend, or disagreements that we cannot resolve. At times like this we do not appear to be quite so competent, self-sufficient, or knowledgeable, and it is embarrassing. It is not easy to admit that "I do not know," or "I can't do that." Like the Israelites, we do not enjoy the wilderness and often long for the "good old days."

The whole congregation of the sons of Israel grumbled against Moses and Aaron in the wilderness. And the sons of Israel said to them, "Would that we had died by the LORD's hand in the land of Egypt, when we sat by the pots of meat, when we ate bread to the full; for you have brought us out into this wilderness to kill this whole assembly with hunger." (Exodus 16:2–3)

When we are given food or rent money or answers to our problems, it is a gift from a source that we do not understand and cannot control, and we query God, as did the Israelites about manna.

When the sons of Israel saw it, they said to one another, "What is it?" For they did not know what it was. (Exodus 16:15)

We are fed what we do not understand so that we *do* come to understand something crucially important, namely, that God alone is the true source of our sustenance. If we fail to understand His Word, we lack a true understanding of what life is all about and a true appreciation of His gifts to us, and can never live life to its fullest.

It is also humbling when clothes do not wear out. The high quality of items at the AmVets store demonstrates that we wish our things would wear out more quickly than they do, so that they can be replaced with the latest and best. If we truly cared for the needy we would keep our usable items for ourselves and buy nice items for them. Wearing new clothes gives us a sense of self-worth, but there is no prestige in wearing last year's styles, or hand-me-down clothing.

We enjoy receiving gifts if they are in appreciation of us or of something we did. If the gift is a handout, desperately needed and totally undeserved or unearned, it is much harder to accept. There is not much pride in being a skid row bum, or a homeless mother. Neither is it easy to live in total dependence on gifts from other people, as must missionaries. Yet, the reason God takes us through the wilderness is to teach us to view His gifts to us as handouts, because that is exactly what God's grace to us is.

The blessing of difficulty is that *difficulty helps us to understand the true nature of God's gifts* to us and it *helps us to rely on Him to provide our needs.*

The wilderness experience is never intended to be permanent. Rather it is intended to prepare us to receive blessing. What's so hard about handling blessing, you might ask. What further preparation could possibly be needed? I'm ready right now!

In reality, it is perhaps more difficult to live with blessing than to live with difficulty. Moses warns us of some of the difficulties of blessing.

"Beware lest you forget the LORD your God by not keeping His commandments and His ordinances and His statutes which I am commanding you today; lest, when you have eaten and are satisfied, and have built good houses and lived in them, and when your herds and your flocks multiply, and your silver and gold multiply, and all that you have multiplies, then your heart becomes proud, and you forget the LORD your God who brought you out from the land of Egypt, out of the house of slavery." (Deuteronomy 8:11–14)

The difficulty with blessing is with our tendency to take credit for what God has done.

The problem is that it is so easy to take blessing and prosperity for granted and to forget the God who gave the blessing. We become satisfied, then self-satisfied, then prideful, and finally complacent about remembering God. When there is a struggle to survive, we are more likely to keep God in our remembrance.

Moses' command to us is to not forget where we have been. Don't forget the hard times! For me, there was the hot summer I lived in a small $8.00 per week room in a run-down neighborhood in east-side Detroit, eating stew out of cans heated with an immersion heater; there were the mornings waiting in line with other indigents at the job service in downtown Cleveland hoping to be hired to dig ditches for a day. There was the day I left college in Cleveland to hitchhike to my parents' home in Florida with $1.35 to my name, and the innumerable boxes of macaroni and cheese (costing 11 cents per box!) that my wife and I ate after we were first married. Remember these times, Moses says, because then, as now, God provided for you and there is no reason for you to become proud.

"Otherwise, you might say in your heart, 'My power and the strength of my hand made me this wealth.' But you shall remember the LORD your God, for it is He who is giving you power to make wealth, that He may confirm His covenant which He swore to your fathers, as it is this day." (Deuteronomy 8:17–18)

The next thing that happens is that we become *self*-confident, believing that we are responsible for all the success we have had. I am well aware that our culture teaches that we need more self-confidence, and that we need to build self-esteem in people, but our culture is wrong. None of our abilities, whether they be creativity, communication skills, good memory, steady hands, or athletic prowess, come from within ourselves. They come from God, and the continual command of Scripture is that we place our full confidence in God, not in ourselves.

If I am successful in a venture, it is only because God gave me success. Nebuchadnezzar, king of Babylon, had to learn this lesson the hard way. He was feeling rather successful and pleased with his accomplishments, when he received a strongly worded reminder of the truth.

The king reflected and said, "Is this not Babylon the great, which I myself have built as a royal residence by the might of my power and for the glory of my majesty?" (Daniel 4:30)

Even though he had played a leading role in the construction of Babylon, he misunderstood that role.

While the word was in the king's mouth, a voice came from heaven, saying, "King Nebuchadnezzar, to you it is declared: sovereignty has been removed from you . . . . until you recognize that the Most High is ruler over the realm of mankind, and bestows it on whomever He wishes." (Daniel 4:31–32)

It is not within your power to determine how successful or prosperous you will be. God alone determines that. Jeremiah told Baruch, his personal secretary (he took dictation from Jeremiah) not to seek success.

"But you, are you seeking great things for yourself? Do not seek them; for behold, I am going to bring disaster on all flesh, " declares the LORD. (Jeremiah 45:5)

An excellent example of this principle is Mark Eaton, for ten years the starting center for the Utah Jazz basketball team. Mark Eaton is 7'4" and has marginal natural athletic ability, at least compared to other professional athletes. He worked extremely hard to develop the skills that he has. But it was because he is 7'4" tall that he was paid over one million dollars a year to play basketball. If he were 6'5" tall with all else the same, he would (by his own admission) have been a car mechanic. Mark Eaton did nothing at all to become 7'4" tall, except eat as his appetite demanded. When he was a young boy he did not decide that he would grow up to be a center in the NBA. Although his father is 6'8" and his mother is 6'1" his parents did not decide that they would have a son who would grow up to be 7'4" tall. Much to the chagrin of many parents today, they have no control over how tall, attractive, smart, or rich their offspring will be. My parents have often joked with me that they thought they had brought the wrong baby home from the hospital when they later realized that I had an above-average ability in mathematics. There was no way they could have predicted or planned it. My success with mathematics, Mark Eaton's height, and your abilities and successes as well, are the gifts of God.

A few years ago I wrote a graduate mathematics textbook. From this experience I learned some things about my so-called accomplishments. First, there was nothing I could do to guarantee that it would be a good book. I put my best effort into the task, and thought long and hard about the correct choice of words and helpful use of examples. It was about the best I could do, but no matter how hard I tried, I could never be certain that the book was good. When God creates something, as He did at the beginning of the universe, He is able to objectively conclude that "it is good"; I have never been justified to have that kind of confidence with my own creation.

Furthermore, I lacked the ideas to know how to make the book better. It was beyond my ability to be witty like Mark Twain, intriguing like Sherlock Holmes, or profound like C. S. Lewis. No matter how I tried I was limited in what I could do. The same God who gave me my abilities also set their limits.

Next, I learned that there was nothing I could do to control the sale of the book. I did not know if students would like it or if professors would order it. Advertising would help, but the acceptance of the book was totally beyond my control. We certainly know of bad books that have sold millions and good books that only collect dust in the warehouse. There are best-selling Christian authors whose works were rejected by numerous publishers before they received their first acceptance.

God was, and is, in complete control of the outcome of my work.

The third thing that happens when we forget God, is that we begin to believe that we deserve our success. We feel that we are inherently better than the competition, and somehow more deserving than they. The Israelites were warned about these kinds of feelings toward the giants in the land of Canaan who were to be overthrown during the conquest.

"Do not say in your heart when the LORD your God has driven them out before you, 'Because of my righteousness the LORD has brought me in to possess this land.'" (Deuteronomy 9:4)

Twice more (Deuteronomy 9:5–6), Moses says explicitly, *it is not because of your righteousness that the LORD your God is giving you this land to possess.*

God does not fight our battles for us or give us a life full of the benefits of His inheritance because we are better, more righteous, or more deserving than other people. He gives these things to us solely because by His grace we are His chosen, adopted children. Yet how often after we receive a bonus or a forgotten tax refund are our first thoughts of ourselves and the expensive toy we want because, "After all, I'm worth it"? Could it be that God is blessing us so that we will have a greater opportunity to be of service to someone else, or to become involved in supporting some special project?

Let's summarize this. Moses tells us that, as part of our inheritance as children of God, heirs of God's kingdom, and in fulfillment of His promise, God wants to provide us with rich, meaningful lives. A key to obtaining the full benefit of this inheritance is to live in obedience to God, and to allow Him to fight our battles for us. However, it is easier to rely on Him when we know that there is nowhere else to turn, when our needs are most obvious to us. This is why we need to experience the wilderness.

When we experience blessing there are three threats that could ruin it all. We have tendencies to forget that God is the source of all we have, to take the credit for our success, and to become self-righteous, believing that we deserved it all anyway. When this happens, it all falls apart, as God no longer fights our battles for us, and we no longer enjoy the full benefits of being His children.

Moses' final words to the nation of Israel indicate that the options are entirely up to you. You alone decide if you want to live in a wilderness, or in the land of promise. In the wilderness, you are wandering about with no real direction or purpose, not able to comprehend the source of the real food of life, and constantly harassed by your enemies. When you choose to live in the land of promised inheritance, you are satisfied with the true bread and water of life, and God fights your battles for you. The choice boils down to one issue, and that is this: Will you or will you not decide to live a life that is in obedience to God Almighty? You choose.

"For this commandment which I command you today is not too difficult for you, nor is it out of reach. . . . I call heaven and earth to witness against you today, that I have set before you life and death, the blessing and the curse. So choose life in order that you may live, you and your descendants, by loving the LORD your God, by obeying His voice, and by holding fast to Him; for this is your life and the length of your days." (Deuteronomy 30:11, 19–20)

It's your life! No one else gets to make your decisions for you. So choose to live in love and obedience of God, and receive in return His free gift of protection and direction. By making this choice, you have learned to count.

Study Guide for Chapter 14

1. For content:
• Read Deuteronomy 8.

• Why does God allow times of difficulty? (Deuteronomy 8:2–5, 15–16)

• What are the pitfalls of the "good times"? (Deuteronomy 8:11–14, 17)

2. For further study:
• In Deuteronomy 6:10–12, Moses gave the warning to "watch yourself" because of what two natural tendencies?

• According to 1 Timothy 6:17, what temptation faces people who are financially blessed and what are they reminded to do?

• At the end of Moses' life, Joshua and the Israelites were instructed to trust God with their future. But apparently there was a problem because one particular phrase of instruction was repeated six times (Deuteronomy 31:1–8, 23; Joshua 1:5–9). What is the phrase and what problem does it suggest? How does Joshua 1:8 address this problem?

3. For application:
• Put into your own words and in a modern context the promise "that you may live and multiply, and go in and possess the land."

• Describe a recent situation in which you could not understand what was happening, and in which you were figuratively "fed manna."

4. For action:
Build your own monument as a way to commemorate God's blessing in your life and in the life of your family. Be creative. For example,

put a small piece of paper describing the occasion of an answered prayer or a special blessing into a "blessings bottle," or light a special candle on the annual date of your child's dedication or christening. Show or describe your monument to your study partners.

5. For personal commitment:
10-forever: Take one of the 10-for-10 commitments you made earlier in this book, and keep up the practice for the rest of your life.

Epilogue

The headline read "College Professor's Proven Formula to Win Lottery Millions." Without reading further, I knew that it was a lie. Aside from the fact that I know something about probability theory, and the fact that this headline was on the front page of the *National Enquirer* (not known as the most reliable source of information), I figured that if this guy really knew how to win millions of dollars in the lottery he would be described as a "former" professor.

Not all of the lies in our society are so blatant. Some are quite subtle. Even so, I am constantly amazed at the lies and falsehoods that people believe. I guess it should not be so surprising, as the Bible says that Christians must "through practice have their senses trained to discern good and evil."

The apostle Paul warned, "Do not be deceived," (1 Corinthians 6:9; Galatians 6:7; Ephesians 5:5–6), and Jesus, when discussing His return warned, "See to it that no one misleds you" (Matthew 24:4; Mark 13:5; Luke 21:8).

Bumper stickers and T-shirts are a pretty good indicator of what people believe about life. I'm sure you've seen the slogans, "Just do it," "If it feels good, do it," and, "Are we having fun yet?"

I hope that you have learned from these studies that these summaries of pop theology are based on lies.

You can't just do it. Everything that you are, every ability you have, and every success you achieve is a gift from God. You can't decide to have a good idea or change someone else's mind. You can't decide to be a great athlete or a famous scientist. The only resources that are truly reliable are God's.

If it feels good, so what? Momentary pleasure is a poor indicator of right or wrong, and a poor substitute for the eternal joy that is available from a lasting relationship with God. "In Thy presence are pleasures forever more." One thing you can be sure of, however, is that living in violation of God's plan is ultimately a pretty miserable way to live.

You're not having fun yet, that is, as long as your number one goal is to please yourself. The deepest pleasures in life come from being obedient to God, seeking to serve others rather than yourself, and praising and honoring Him in all that you do.

Note to the Reader

The publisher invites you to share your response to the message of this book by writing Discovery House Publishers, P. O. Box 3566, Grand Rapids, MI 49501, U.S.A. or by calling 1-800-653-8333. For information about other Discovery House publications, contact us at the same address and phone number.